The Knitted Teddy Bear

Make Your Own Heirloom Toys, with Dozens of Patterns for Unique Clothing

The Knitted Teddy Bear

Make Your Own Heirloom Toys, with Dozens of Patterns for Unique Clothing

Sandra Polley

COLLINS & BROWN

First published in the United Kingdom in 2004
First published in paperback in 2010 by
Collins & Brown
10 Southcombe Street
London W14 0RA

An imprint of Anova Books Company Ltd

Photography by Sian Irvine and Michael Wicks

ISBN 978-1-84340-595-5

A CIP catalogue for this book is available from the British Library.

10 9 8 7 6 5 4 3 2 1

Reproduction by Rival Colour Ltd, UK
Printed and bound by 1010 Printing International Ltd, China

This book can be ordered direct from the publisher at
www.anovabooks.com

Sandra Polley has had many years experience with crafts,
especially knitting and soft toy making. She started to design
her traditionally-styled knitted bears about 6 years ago and
now runs a successful small business selling her patterns
through wool shops and haberdashery's around the UK.

Safety Note
*Do not use small beads or buttons on bears intended for use
by babies or children under three years old, as they may
cause a choking hazard if swallowed. Even safety eyes are
not completely safe when used with knitted toys.*

Contents

Introduction

I have tried, with this book, to create an absorbing and addictive hobby, and one which will give pleasure to both the maker and the recipient.

It is well known that knitting is very therapeutic and relaxing—you cannot think about your problems too much while counting stitches and rows! There is also the added bonus that you can sit in a comfortable armchair in front of the fire or outside in a deckchair, rather than at a table with various pieces of equipment as with many other crafts.

Teddy bears make wonderful presents, and the gift of a knitted bear, which has been carefully and lovingly made, will be treasured far more than one that has been bought and, chances are, it will still have a loving home long after more commercial toys have been sent to the charity shops. You can always find room for a tiny ted in a suitcase bound for university or travelling.

Bears are very collectable and they are more often chosen for their "take-me-home and love me" look rather than any thoughts as to their quality or future value in monetary terms. Although most are made from mohair or plush, there is often one or two little knitted ones whose homespun charm can't be resisted.

I make no apology for the fact that most of the bears in this book are quite small. As they take up so little room while you are making them, everything fits easily into a shoulder bag and they only take two or three evenings to make. Many little characters can be quickly made for Christmas stockings, charity stalls and fairs.

All of the patterns are easy to follow, with no complicated stitches or designs, and most can be made from quite small amounts of yarn. The clothes and accessories have also been kept to a simple design and are quick and easy to knit.

I hope you will find some good ideas in this book. If you experiment with different yarns, textures and needle sizes, you can create your own quite unique little teds. They don't have to be perfect; they will be well loved just the way they are!

If you enjoy making any of these projects as much as I have, then your time has been well spent and another little bear has been born.

There are little teds and big teds to suit children (and adults!) of all ages, who will cherish their own little knitted friends.

Materials

Yarn

Almost any yarn can be used to make knitted bears, and they are a good way to use up all those oddments left over from other projects. However, the type of yarn used will directly affect the look and size of the bear and your enjoyment of making it.

Yarns with a high content of wool make lovely teddies but the finished pieces are not as easy to sew up as acrylics because of the springiness and tendency of the yarn to curl up at the edges. Therefore you will need to press the pieces well, either under a damp cloth or with some steam, before sewing them together.

Which thickness of yarn to use for each pattern is up to you. I have given the ones which I designed the bears for and which I found the most appropriate but, providing you use suitable sized knitting needles, they can all be adapted to suit your taste.

Embroidery thread

I have found embroidery thread the most suitable thread for sewing the features and claws for my bears. You may like to use knitting yarn or another type of thread, it is a matter of personal taste.

Knitting needles

There are only four sizes of needle used for the bears in this book. If you find that your knitting tension feels too tight or too loose, you can use a larger or smaller size needle as appropriate. Try to find needles which are not too long, a size of 10 inches (25cm) is ideal. If you are keen to make one of the miniature bears even smaller you can use either a US size 0 (2mm) which is the smallest size available from general knitting suppliers, or you can buy even smaller needles from specialty suppliers or teddy or doll fairs. When making the clothes for the bears, always use the same size needles for the bear and the clothes, unless otherwise indicated.

Stuffing

In the past, teddy bears were stuffed with materials such as straw, wood wool or kapok, and during the war years, old pieces of rags and clothes. Nowadays you can buy good quality washable polyester toy filling from haberdashers and craft shops. This stuffing is clean, light, relatively cheap and easy to use. It will also probably have been tested for fire resistance. Amounts of stuffing given are approximate as it is a question of how you wish your finished bear to look as to how much stuffing you use.

Another good source of stuffing can be found in new polyester quilts and pillows, which are relatively inexpensive. Foam chips are not suitable for making small toys as they are lumpy and difficult to use.

Sewing needles

Needles for sewing knitted pieces together have a blunt point to prevent the yarn splitting and a large "eye" to thread the thick yarn through. They are generally called "tapestry," "yarn" or "knitters" needles and they are available in many different sizes. A medium size is adequate for the bears and clothes in the following projects. When making the very small bears you might like to use matching sewing thread and a smaller needle to make a neater seam.

Eyes

The best type of eyes for the small bears like *Annie & George* (page 16) and *Christopher* (page 22) are the specialty looped-back black eyes. These are especially made for teddy bears and can be bought from bear and doll fairs or by mail order from craft suppliers (there is a useful list of addresses at the end of the book). If you cannot get the specialty eyes, black beads are readily available and are also very effective and will bring your bear to life.

Plastic safety eyes for the larger bears can also be found in most sewing and knitting stores.

Forceps or tweezers

These are very useful pieces of equipment and are essential when making the miniature bears. They will help to turn the finished pieces out the right way after sewing up, and they will grip and stuff small amounts of stuffing into all the tiny spaces.

Pins

Coloured plastic-headed pins are best when assembling knitted bears as they are less likely to get accidentally left in your knitting. Black-headed pins are very useful for trying out eye positions (see the panel on page 14 for suggestions).

Scissors

A sharp pair of embroidery scissors is best for snipping off threads. My favorites are little stainless steel, plastic handled ones.

Pencil

Keep a pencil handy to mark where you are when you stop or get disturbed. This saves a lot of time and mistakes and you can always erase the marks afterwards. A pencil is also useful for pushing the stuffing down into noses and paws.

Buttons

There are instructions in this book for making tiny buttons for your teddy's cardigan from modelling clay, which can be baked in a domestic oven (see page 15). You can also buy very small buttons from specialty toy suppliers. Small beads also make sweet buttons for little teds' clothes. Larger, household buttons make very good joints for bears intended for older children or adults.

Row counter

When knitting in garter stitch or with a bouclé-type yarn, it is difficult to see where an increase or decrease row is. A row counter will help you to keep track of where you are. You can buy one that attaches to the end of your needle or sits on the table.

Tape measure

Although most of the instructions state the amount of rows to knit, there are occasionally pieces of work to measure.

General Instructions

Needle sizes

Only the four needle sizes listed below are used in this book.

US Size	Metric Size	Old UK & Canadian Size
3	3¼	10
3	3	11
2	2¾	12
1	2¼	13

Converting weights and lengths

oz	=	g x 0.0352
g	=	oz x 28.35
in	=	cm x 0.3937
cm	=	in x 2.54

Abbreviations

Approx—approximately
st(s)—stitch(es)
K—knit
P—purl
Dec—decrease, by knitting/purling 2 stitches together
Inc—increase, by knitting/purling into the front and back of a stitch
beg—beginning
tog—together
alt—alternate
Rib—K1, P1, across row
Sl 1—slip next stitch
psso—pass slipped stitch over
yfwd—yarn forward
rep—repeat
( )—repeat instructions inside parentheses as instructed

Stitches used

St st—stocking stitch—1 row knit, 1 row pearl
G. st—garter stitch—every row knit
Single rib—knit 1, purl 1, alternately across row
Moss st—knit 1, purl 1 across row, on next row, knit the purl sts and purl the knit sts (a sort of alternating rib)

All the bears can be adapted to knit with fingering, sport weight or worsted (D/K, 3-ply or 4-ply yarn). Chunky yarn is probably too thick for all but the largest bear. Suitable size knitting needles to go with each yarn are given with each pattern instruction but as a general guide US sizes 1 (2¼mm) or 2 (2¾mm) are best with fingering (4-ply yarn) and sizes 2 or 3 (2¾ or 3¼mm) with light worsted (D/K) yarn.

Start all work with a K row unless otherwise stated. All rib throughout the book is single rib (K1, P1).

Using pins

When pinning the pieces of work together, place the pins in at right angles to the seam. This takes up less room and keeps the sharp point of the pin out of the way.

Using markers

Markers may be used to help with sewing up the pieces and a guide for eye positions. Have a yarn needle threaded with a long length of yarn of a different shade to the one you are using. Wherever you need a marker, make a couple of little stitches around 1 knitted stitch and then snip off close to your work. Carefully remove after sewing up.

Ears

Although I have made the ears to the proportions that I think suit each bear, in a lot of cases they are very similar in size and shape to each other, so after making a few bears from this book, you might like to interchange them. For instance, you might find that you prefer Christopher's single thickness ears on Bertie or Thomas, and so on.

Ear

Shaping ears

Before sewing the ears on, use the long thread left attached and make a small running stitch along the very outer edge of the curved part of the ear. Pull slightly and fasten off with a couple more stitches. This will curve the ear slightly and also smooth out any nobbly bits where you have cast off.

Backstitch

This type of stitch makes the neatest seam and is best used for all but the smallest bears. Working on the wrong side of work, with right sides together, take very small backstitches about one stitch in from the edge.

Oversew stitch

This stitch is very straightforward and the best way to sew up all the little bear clothes, as it makes the seams less bulky than with backstitch. It is worked on the wrong side, with right sides together, as with backstitch. Take very small stitches from both edges of work, one from each row and work from back to front and then over to the back again for each stitch.

Ladderstitch

Knot a length of thread and secure it at the edge of the opening in the seam. Take small stitches either side of the open seam, gently pulling the seam closed every three or four stitches to the end. Secure with a couple more stitches.

Darning in threads

Apart from the long thread left at the top of the ears, it is easier to rethread and darn all the loose threads into the edge or back of your work and trim them before sewing up. You might think that they are useful to sew up with but they only get in the way and are usually too short to use anyway.

Casting off

You will see that when casting off at the top of the limbs and some other places, the instructions say either to slip the first stitch or knit 2 together at each end of the row at the same time. This is to help smooth out the shaped edges of the seams and is quite easy to do. Cast off in the usual way but either slip the first stitch on to the right needle first, or knit 2 together, cast off to the last 2 stitches, knit 2 together and cast off last stitch.

Increasing and decreasing

If you were knitting a sweater or cardigan for yourself, your instructions would probably tell you to do the increasing or decreasing 1 stitch in from the edge and the shaping would form part of the overall design of the garment. This method will give a smoother edge and can sometimes be used when working on the body and limbs of your bears (unless otherwise stated). You don't want any shaping to show on your bear's face, so when working on the head or head gusset it is better to increase or decrease in the first and last stitch or stitches.

Any uneven edges will not show if you backstitch the pieces together when sewing up.

Tension

I haven't included a tension square with the instructions because it doesn't really matter if your bear comes out a little bit bigger or smaller than the finished size given. If you know that you are a very loose knitter then use one size smaller needles, or use larger needles if you knit tightly.

However, it is important to use the same brand or thickness of yarn for the clothes as that used for the bear, otherwise they might not fit. Some worsted (double knitting) or fingering (4-ply yarns) are thicker than others and this will make a difference to the finished size.

Having said all that, most of the clothes are so quick to knit up that you could take a chance with some of those oddments that you have left over, and if they don't fit one bear they will probably fit another.

Pressing

After knitting up the pieces, they will usually need pressing before being sewn together.

This might not be necessary if you have used an acrylic yarn but yarns with a high wool content tend to make the knitted pieces curl at the edges which makes it difficult to sew them together.

The pieces for the smaller bears will certainly need a good press, especially if they are to be sewn up with purl sides together to make a reverse stocking stitch bear. The usual way is to pin them out, wrong side facing to a flat pad or the ironing board, and cover them with a damp cloth to press with a warm iron. Instead, I usually set the iron to warm, also with a low steam setting and hover it just above the pieces for a few seconds while they dampen slightly, then press quickly, especially at the edges where they tend to curl in. You do have to be careful but it is a lot quicker once you've mastered it. You could quickly knit up a small square and practise first.

Sewing up the pieces

Always take your time sewing up the pieces and try to work in good light —daylight if possible. I tend to do my knitting in the evening and keep the sewing up for the daytime if I can. If I have to put a bear together at night, I use a halogen sewing lamp. They are relatively expensive, but it is one of the best investments I have made and is extremely useful. After sewing the seams with a backstitch, roll and press them out quite firmly with your finger and thumb to flatten them.

Stuffing

As with all soft toys, how you stuff your bear will directly affect the finished appearance. It is important to stuff firmly, but without stretching the knitting out of place. Always stuff well down into the extremities, such as the nose and paws first, and mould into shape as you go along. A pair of forceps or tweezers, or even a pencil, are very useful for stuffing the smaller bears, especially the miniatures. If you intend to thread-joint your finished bear, put slightly more stuffing in the body as the jointing will pull the body in and decrease its bulk.

The amount of stuffing needed for each bear will vary depending on knitting tension and individual taste, therefore requirements given for each pattern are approximate.

Thread-jointing

First pin the arms and legs to the body. The top of the arms should be positioned a little way down from the top of the body and slightly more towards the back than the front. Check that the tops of the arms are level before finalizing their position.

The top of the legs should be about ½ inch (2 or 3cm) up from teddy's bottom (depending on bear size) but check that he/she can sit correctly. Long doll needles are very useful for trying out limb positions. Put the arms and legs to one side, replacing the pins in the exact position where the limb "joints" are going to be.

To attach the legs, thread a needle with a long piece of extra strong thread, doubled, or alternatively use some body-coloured yarn. Push the needle through one side of the body at the pin position (leaving a long thread) through one leg, back into the leg through the same hole you came out of, coming out of the inside of the leg a couple of stitches away. Then go back through the body and into the second leg and back into the

Attaching the limbs.

same hole of this leg as before, bringing the needle out between the leg and the body (back to where you started). Pull the threads tightly, knot, then rethread and sink ends into the body out of sight. Attach the arms in the same way.

Sewing on limbs

You may not want to thread-joint, if, for example, the bear is for a younger child. Pin the limbs to the body as before. Then, using bear-coloured yarn, take a few stitches from the inside of the arms and legs (about ½ inch or 1cm down from the top edge) and go through the body to the corresponding limbs. Pull the yarn each time so that the limbs fit snugly into the body. Do this several times until everything is secure.

Attaching the eyes.

Adding the eyes

First, decide how you want your finished bear to look—the eyes you use can make a huge difference here. There are two main types—looped-back teddy eyes, available from craft stores, or small beads. They are both inserted in the same way.

Cut a piece of strong black thread about 6–8 inches (15–20cm) long and thread one end through an 'eye' and then onto your tapestry needle. Push the needle down into the chosen position of one eye and bring it out at the back of the neck, pulling a couple of inches of thread (see below). Be careful not to lose the bead from the other end of the thread at this time. Rethread the other end of the thread and push the needle down into the head very close to the first entry hole, again coming out at the back of the neck, and securing the eye. Repeat with the other eye, then pull each pair of threads to embed the eyes a slightly, knot them together securely, trim and sink the ends into the head. Try out different positions to get them right.

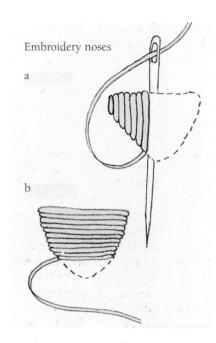

Embroidery noses

a

b

Sewing claws

You will need some black or brown embroidery thread or yarn for sewing the claws. Usually two or three strands is the right thickness.

Cut a length of thread, about 8–10 inches (20–25 cm) long, and knot one end. Take the needle and thread into the paw, coming out at the beginning of the first claw and pulling the thread until the knotted end disappears into the paw. Make three "claws" in the same way, and then pull the needle out further up the limb. Push it back in exactly the same place, come back out a little further away, pull the thread to create some tension, snip off close to the surface and the thread should disappear into the bear.

Sewing noses and mouths

Noses for teddy bears are usually sewn in satin stitch, with the threads running either vertically (a) or horizontally (b)—see left. A variety of different shapes can be embroidered onto the larger mohair bears, but for our little knitted teds, a small neat triangle is quite adequate. You can either stitch the nose and mouth all in one go with the same thread, or do the nose first and then sew the mouth with a fresh piece of thread afterwards. As I quite often change my mind about the mouth several times for each bear, I find it is better to do it separately and have only a couple of stitches to undo if necessary, rather than having to start all over.

Although the mouth itself is only two or three stitches, how you place it will have a big impact on your bear's face and you may have to experiment a bit before you get the look you want.

Some ideas are given on the right which may be of help when choosing your bear's personality.

Aftercare

Whether or not you wash your little bears is really down to commonsense. Make sure that the stuffing you use is washable. Smaller bears can be hand-washed quickly, gently squeezed in a towel to remove excess water and dried in a well-ventilated area. The larger bears are probably best surface-cleaned with a damp cloth, rather than being completely submerged in water.

Facial expressions

Slightly larger eyes will make teddy look younger.

Smaller eyes, set further away from the nose will give an older look.

To give your bear a quizzical look, set the eyes closer together inside the gusset seam.

Sometimes it's nice to have a bear with a nice big smile!

How to make buttons

You can make your own tiny buttons for teddy bear cardigans and sweaters from Fimo (or similar) modelling clay, which can be bought from craft and modelling shops and comes in a large range of colours.

All the equipment you need is an oven tray, access to an oven, and a tapestry or wool needle.

Break off a small amount of clay, about ¾ inch (2cm) square, and knead it for a few minutes until smooth. Then take off a tiny little piece, the size of a pin head, roll it into a ball and press it gently onto the oven tray to flatten it.

Repeat this process a few times to get accustomed to the process and because inevitably, some pieces will be bigger than others, you will need to pick out the ones that are the closest in size to each other.

When you have got enough buttons, take the tapestry needle and, without moving them, carefully press two holes next to each other in the centre of each button, twisting the needle around a couple of times to widen the hole slightly. Preheat the oven to the temperature instructed on the modelling clay packet, then put the oven tray and buttons in to bake. You may find that they need five minutes less than the instructions given because they are so small. When they are ready, leave them for about ten minutes to cool, then gently lift or slide them off with a knife.

It does not matter if the holes haven't gone right through the buttons, as the needle and thread should easily push through the last little bit when you come to sew them on to your bear.

Remember, whichever teddies you make, do not add buttons or any small pieces to teddy garments intended for babies or small children as they may cause a choking hazard if swallowed.

Annie & George

These little bears have fully moveable joints and contrast paw pads. They look very cute in their his 'n' hers sweaters. After knitting the pieces, sew them up with purl sides together to make reverse stocking stitch bears.

Materials
- Approx **1oz ball fingering (30g 4-ply) yarn** in the colour of your choice for each bear
- Approx **1oz ball fingering (30g 4-ply) yarn** in a contrasting shade for the paw pads
- Approx **1oz ball fingering (30g 4-ply) yarn** in the colour of your choice for the sweaters
- A pair of **US 2 (2¾mm) knitting needles**
- **2 small black beads or 4mm looped-back teddy eyes**
- Strong **black thread** for attaching bead or teddy eyes
- Approx ½oz (10g) polyester **stuffing** for each bear
- A **tapestry or wool needle** for sewing up bear
- **Black or brown and white embroidery thread** for eyes, nose, mouth and claws
- **Forceps or tweezers** for turning and stuffing bear (optional)
- **Safety pin** or stitch holder for working neckband of sweaters
- **1 x 6mm press fasteners** for each sweater

The bears shown are knitted in Paton 4-ply Natural (4283) with sweaters of Paton 4-ply in Pink (4219) and Blue (4220). Paton Soft camel (4292) has been used for the paw pads.

Height
Approximately 7 inches (18 cm).

Work in St st throughout unless otherwise stated. The bears will then be sewn up Purl sides together to make reverse stocking stitch bears.

Head and Body
Side A
make 1
With main colour, cast on 8 sts
Starting with a K row:
ROW 1—Inc 1 st at each end of row (10 sts)
ROW 2—P
ROW 3—(Inc 1, K2) 3 times, Inc in last st (14 sts)
ROW 4—P
ROW 5—Inc 1, K3, Inc 1, K4, Inc 1, K3, Inc 1 (18 sts)
St st 9 rows, (ending on a P row)
ROW 15—Dec 1 st at beg of row
St st 7 rows
ROW 23—Inc 1 st at beg of row
ROW 24—P
ROW 25—Dec 1 st at end of row and following 2 alt rows (15 sts)
ROW 30—P
ROW 31—K2 tog, K2, K2 tog, K3, K2 tog, K2, K2 tog (11 sts)
ROW 32—P
ROW 33—Dec 1 st at each end of row (9 sts)

To shape head and neck
ROW 34—P
ROW 35—K
ROW 36—Cast on 4 sts at beg of row, and P across this row
ROW 37—Inc 1 st at each end of row (15 sts)
ROW 38—P
ROW 39—Inc 1 st at end of row (16 sts)
St st 4 rows
ROW 44—Cast off 2 sts at beg of row
ROW 45—Dec 1 st at end of row
ROW 46—Cast off 2 sts at beg of row, slipping the first st (11 sts)
ROW 47—Dec 1 st at each end of row
ROW 48—P
ROW 49—Dec 1 st at each end of row and following row (5 sts)
Cast off

Head and Body
Side B
make 1
With main colour, cast on 8 sts, starting with a P row:
ROW 1—Inc 1 st at each end of row (10 sts)
ROW 2—K
ROW 3—(Inc 1, P2) 3 times, Inc in last st (14 sts)
ROW 4—K
ROW 5—Inc 1, P3, Inc 1, P4, Inc 1, P3, Inc 1 (18 sts)
St st 9 rows (ending on a K row)
ROW 15—Dec 1 st at beg of row
St st 7 rows

ROW 23—Inc 1 st at beg of row

ROW 24—K

ROW 25—Dec 1 st at end of row and following 2 alt rows (15 sts)

ROW 30—K

ROW 31—P2 tog, P2, P2 tog, P3, P2 tog, P2, P2 tog. (11 sts)

ROW 32—K

ROW 33—Dec 1 st at each end of row (9 sts)

To shape head and neck

ROW 34—K

ROW 35—P

ROW 36—Cast on 4 sts at beg of row, and K across this row

ROW 37—Inc 1 st at each end of row (15 sts)

ROW 38—K

ROW 39—Inc 1 st at end of row (16 sts)

St st 4 rows, (ending on a P row)

ROW 44—Cast off 2 sts at beg of row

ROW 45—Dec 1 st at end of row

ROW 46—Cast off 2 sts at beg of row, slipping the first st (11 sts)

ROW 47—Dec 1 st at each end of row

ROW 48—K

ROW 49—Dec 1 st at each end of row and following row (5 sts)

Cast off, slipping the first st

Head Gusset
make 1

Starting at nose

With main colour, cast on 4 sts

Starting with a K row:

ROW 1—Inc 1 st at each end of row (6 sts)

St st 5 rows

ROW 7—Inc 1 st at each end of row and following 2 alt rows (12 sts)

St st 14 rows

ROW 26—Dec 1 st at each end of every row until 2 sts

K2 tog and finish off

Ears
make 2

With main colour, cast on 8 sts.

Working in G. st:

K 2 rows

Dec 1 st at each end of next and following alt row (4 sts)

Cast off, slipping the first st and leaving a long thread (to sew ear to head)

Outside Arm
Side A
make 1

With main colour, cast on 3 sts

Starting with a K row:

ROW 1—Inc 1 st at each end of row and following alt row (7 sts)

ROW 4—P

ROW 5—Inc 1 st at end of row (8 sts)

ROW 6—P

ROW 7—Dec 1 st at beg and Inc 1 st at end of row

ROW 8—P

ROW 9 AND 10—Rep the last 2 rows **

St st 6 rows

ROW 17—Inc 1 st at end of row (9 sts)

St st 12 rows (ending on a K row)

ROW 30—Dec 1 st at each end of row and following alt row (5 sts)

Cast off, slipping the first st

Outside Arm
Side B
make 1

With main colour, cast on 3 sts

Starting with a K row:

ROW 1—Inc 1 st at each end of row and following alt row (7 sts)

ROW 4—P

ROW 5—Inc 1 st at beg of row (8 sts)

ROW 6—P

ROW 7—Inc 1 st at beg and Dec 1 st at end of row

ROW 8—P

ROW 9 AND 10—Rep the last 2 rows **

St st 6 rows

ROW 17—Inc 1 st at beg of row (9 sts)

Complete as for outer arm, side A

Inside Arms

Working in contrast colour, follow instructions as for each outer arm to **

NEXT ROW—K

NEXT ROW—change to main colour and K, (knitting instead of purling this row prevents a joining line showing)

St st 4 rows, starting with a K row

Complete as for rest of outer arm (from row 17)

Legs
make 2

With main colour, cast on 28 sts

ROW 1—P

ROW 2—Dec 1 st at each end of row and following 2 alt rows (22 sts)

ROW 7—P

ROW 8—Cast off 3 sts at beg of row and following row

ROW 10—Inc 1 st at each end of row and following 8 th row (20 sts)

St st 7 rows

ROW 26—K2 tog, K6, K2 tog twice, K6, K2 tog

ROW 27—P
ROW 28—K2 tog, K4, K2 tog twice.
Cast off in P

Soles
make 2

With contrast colour, cast on 3 sts. Starting with a k row:
ROW 1—Inc 1 st at each end of row and following alt row (7 sts)
St st 10 rows, ending on a k row
ROW 14—Dec 1 st at each end of row and following alt row (3 sts)
Cast off, slipping the first st.

To make up

Press all the pieces on the purl side with a warm iron, especially at the edges where they tend to curl in, then match all pieces P sides together to sew up.

Head and Body— (see diagram)

Pin the two head and body pieces together. To sew, use a small backstitch and sew about 1 st in from the edge. Starting from the nose (a), work around the chin, neck, tummy and bottom to the middle of the back (b). Pin the head gusset to both sides of the nose, starting at the nose and working around to the back of the head (c), adjusting to fit and making sure both sides are even. Sew in using backstitch as before, and then sew about ¾ inch (2cm) down the neck and shoulders (d).
You should now have a gap in the back for turning and stuffing.

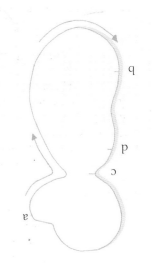

Turn and stuff carefully, starting with the nose and head, moulding into shape as you go. Make sure the nose area is well stuffed first. Stuff the head and body firmly but be careful not to overstuff or your knitting may pull out of shape.
When you are happy with the shape of your bear, close the back opening using ladderstitch. Tie a piece of the same colour yarn around the neck and pull firmly to define the neck and shoulders. Tie a knot and sink the ends of the yarn into the body out of sight.

Ears

Sew in and trim off the shorter cast on thread. Thread the longer thread onto the needle; weave it in along the edge of the ear down to the corner and pull slightly to give a nice rounded shape. Take a couple of sts

to anchor the thread and use the rest to sew the ears to the head. Pin in position first, about ¼ inch (1cm) from the back of the head and about halfway across the head gusset seam. This is only a guide; you may like to experiment with the ear positions before sewing them on.

Eyes

If you are giving this bear to a child, make two or three tiny stitches on top of each other with black or brown embroidery thread or yarn in each eye position. One tiny stitch in white thread over the top will bring the eyes to life.
Looped-back teddy eyes or beads—see General instructions on page 13.

Nose and Mouth

Using two or three strands of black or brown embroidery thread, sew a triangle in satin st for the nose and work three little stitches for the mouth.

Arms

Match the pairs of arms (purl together), pin and sew, leaving a small gap at the back for turning and stuffing. Turn out and stuff carefully, check they match in size and then close gap.

To make up first sew from "a" to "b". Position head gusset and sew from "a" to "c", and sew from "c" to "d", on both sides, leaving a gap between "d" and "b" for turning and stuffing.

Legs

Fold each leg in half lengthways (P sides together), pin and sew, leaving the bottom edges open and a small gap at the front for turning and stuffing. Pin, adjust, and sew the soles to the feet. Turn out and stuff carefully, using very small amounts of stuffing at a time. Check that each leg matches the other in size, then sew up the gap in the seams, using ladderstitch.

Claws

With two strands of black or brown embroidery thread or yarn, make three claws on all four paws. To make the claws knot the end of a length of thread. Take the needle and thread into the paw, coming out at the beginning of the first claw and pulling the thread until the knotted end disappears into the paw.

Make three claws in this way and then pull the needle out further up the limb. Push the needle back in exactly the same hole, come back out a bit further away, pull the thread to create some tension, snip off close to the surface and the thread should disappear into the bear.

To thread-joint your bear—see General Instructions on page 13.

If you don't want to thread-joint your bear, or it needs extra strength as a child's toy, first pin the limbs to the body in the same positions as before. Then, using bear-coloured yarn, take a few stitches from the inside of the tops of the arms and

legs and go through the body to the corresponding limb, pulling the yarn firmly each time so that the limbs fit snugly into the body. Do this two or three times until you are happy that they are secure. Try not to spread the stitches out too much or there will not be much range of movement in the limbs.

Sweater

Work in St st throughout unless otherwise stated.

Front

With colour of choice, cast on 25 sts
Work 2 rows single rib
Beg with a K row, St st 8 rows **
Mark each end of last row with a coloured thread

To shape armholes

Dec 1 st at each end of next and every alt row until 9 sts remain
NEXT ROW—P
Leave sts on a holder for now

Back

Cast on 25 sts
Work as front until **
Mark each end of last row with a coloured thread

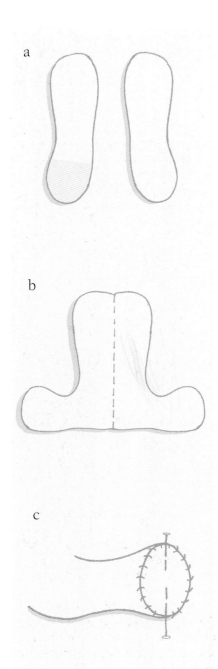

Match the arms (a), leaving a space for the stuffing. Fold the legs lengthways (b) before sewing in the soles of the feet (c) and turning the right way out.

To shape armholes and back opening

NEXT ROW—Dec 1 st at each end of row

NEXT ROW—P

NEXT ROW—K2 tog, K10, turn and work on these sts for now

NEXT ROW—K2, P to end

NEXT ROW—K2 tog, K to end

Rep the last 2 rows until 5 sts remain

NEXT ROW—K2, P to end, leave these sts on a holder for now

With right side facing, rejoin yarn to remaining sts, cast on 2 sts at beg of row and K to last 2 sts, K2 tog.

NEXT ROW—P to last 2 sts, K2

Continue to dec on every K row keeping G. st edge correct until 7 sts remain, leave these sts on a holder for now.

Sleeves
make 2

Cast on 17 sts and rib 2 rows

St st 2 rows

NEXT ROW—Inc 1 st at each end of row and following 2 alt rows (23 sts). Mark each end of last row.

To shape top of sleeves

St st 3 rows, (ending on a P row)

NEXT ROW—Dec 1 st at each end of row and every alt row until 7 sts remain

NEXT ROW—P

Leave sts on a holder for now

To make up

Join all raglan seams. With right sides facing, rib across sts on holder in the following order:

Left back, left sleeve, front, right sleeve, right back. Rib 1 further row, then cast off in rib. It is a bit difficult as there isn't much room to manoeuvre, a safety pin or st holder would be useful.

Sew up the rest of the seams. Overlap the rib opening at the back of the neck and catch down with a few sts. Sew on a press fastener at the back of neck.

Christopher & Rosie

Here are two well–fed, happy little bears, all ready to go out to play in their overalls. They have long bodies and arms and quite short legs. They could be collector's bears or toys for a child if the eyes are embroidered.

Materials

- Approx **2oz fingering (50g 4-ply) yarn** in the colour of your choice for each bear
- Approx **1oz fingering (30g 4-ply) yarn** of a contrast colour for paw pads and soles
- Approx **1oz fingering (30g 4-ply) yarn** in the colour of your choice for the overalls
- **2 small buttons** for the overalls
- A pair of **US 2 (2¾mm)** knitting needles
- Approx **1 oz (28g) of polyester stuffing**
- **2 small black beads**, 2 x ¼ inch (4mm) looped-back eyes, or a length of black embroidery yarn for the eyes
- **Strong black thread** for attaching beads or teddy eyes
- A **tapestry or wool needle** for sewing up bear
- Black or dark brown **embroidery thread** for nose, mouth and claws

The bears shown are knitted in Paton 4-ply Natural (4823) with overalls in Denim (4136) and Hollyhock (4258).

Height

Approximately 9 inches (23cm).

Work in St st throughout unless otherwise stated.

Body and Head
Side A
make 1

With main colour, cast on 9 sts
Starting with a K row, Inc 1 st at each end of every row until 19 sts
ROW 6—P
ROW 7—(Inc 1, K5), 3 times, Inc 1 (23 sts)
ROW 8—P
ROW 9—Inc 1 st at end of row
St st 11 rows (ending on a P row)
ROW 21—Dec 1 st at beg of row and following alt row (22 sts)
St st 3 rows
ROW 27—Dec 1 st at beg of row (21 sts)
ROW 28—P
ROW 29—Dec 1 st at end of row (20 sts)
St st 3 rows
Rep last 4 rows (19 sts)
ROW 37—Inc 1 st at beg and dec 1 st at end of row
ROW 38—P
ROW 39—Dec 1 st at end of row and each alt row until 15 sts
ROW 46—P
ROW 47—Dec 1 st at each end of row and following alt row (11 sts)
ROW 50—Dec 1 st at end of row
St st 2 rows, ending on a P row

To shape head

ROW 53—Inc 1 st at end of row
ROW 54—Cast on 4 sts, P to end
ROW 55—Inc 1 st at end of row (16 sts)
ROW 56—Inc 1 st at beg of row
ROW 57—Inc 1 st at end of row (18 sts)
St st 7 rows (ending on a P row)
ROW 65—Dec 1 st at beg of row

To shape nose

ROW 66—Cast off 5 sts, P to last 2 sts, P2 tog
ROW 67—Dec 1 st at each end of row and following row (7 sts)
Cast off, knitting 2 sts tog at each end of row at same time

Body and Head
Side B
make 1

With main colour, cast on 9 sts
Starting with a P row, Inc 1 st at each end of every row until 19 sts
ROW 6—K
ROW 7—(Inc 1, P5), 3 times, Inc 1 (23 sts)
ROW 8—K
ROW 9—Inc 1 st at end of row
St st 11 rows (ending on a K row)
ROW 21—Dec 1 st at beg of row and following alt row
St st 3 rows
ROW 27—Dec 1 st at beg of row (21 sts)
ROW 28—K
ROW 29—Dec 1 st at end of row (20 sts)
St st 3 rows

Rep last 4 rows (19 sts)

ROW 37—1 st at beg and Dec 1 st at end of row

ROW 38—K

ROW 39—Dec 1 st at end of row and each alt row until 15 sts

ROW 46—K

ROW 47—Dec 1 st at each end of row and following alt row (11 sts)

ROW 50—Dec 1 st at end of row

St st 2 rows, ending on a K row

To shape head

ROW 53—Inc 1 st at end of row

ROW 54—Cast on 4 sts, K to end (15 sts)

ROW 55—Inc 1 st at end of row

ROW 56—Inc 1 st at beg of row

ROW 57—Inc 1 st at end of row (18 sts)

St st 7 rows (ending on a K row)

ROW 65—Dec 1 st at beg of row

To shape nose

ROW 66—Cast off 5 sts, K to last 2 sts, K2 tog

ROW 67—Dec 1 st at each end of row and following row (7 sts)

Cast off in P, working 2 sts tog at each end of row at the same time

Head Gusset

make 1

With main colour, cast on 3 sts

P 1 row

Inc 1 st at each end of row and every alt row until 13 sts

St st 9 rows (ending on a P row)

To shape nose

Dec 1 st at each end of next 3 rows (7 sts)

St st 7 rows

K2 tog at each end of row

Cast off in P

Ears

make 2

With main colour cast on 8 sts, working in G. st:

K4 rows

Dec 1 st at each end of row and following alt row

K2 tog twice and cast off in same row, leaving a long thread (to sew ears to head)

Outside Arm

side A

make 1

With main colour, cast on 3 sts

Starting with a K row:

ROW 1—Inc 1 st at each end of this and every row until 9 sts

ROW 4—P

ROW 5—Inc 1 st at beg of row and following 2 alt rows (12 sts)

ROW 10—P

ROW 11—Inc 1 st at beg and Dec 1 st at end of row

ROW 12—P **

ROW 13—Dec 1 st at end of row and following alt row (10 sts)

ROW 16—Dec 1 st at beg of row

ROW 17—Inc 1 st at beg of row (10 sts)

St st 7 rows (ending on a P row)

Rep last 8 rows twice (12 sts)

Dec 1 st at each end of next 3 rows (6 sts)

Cast off, taking 2 sts tog at each end of row at same time

Outside Arm

side B

make 1

With main colour, cast on 3 sts

Starting with a K row:

ROW 1—Inc 1 st at each end of this and every row until 9 sts

ROW 4—P

ROW 5—Inc 1 st at end of row and following 2 alt rows (12 sts)

ROW 10—P

ROW 11—Dec 1 st at beg and Inc 1 st at end of row

ROW 12—P **

ROW 13—Dec 1 st at beg of row and following alt row (10 sts)

ROW 16—Dec 1 st at end of row

ROW 17—Inc 1 st at end of row (10 sts)

St st 7 rows (ending on a P row)

Rep last 8 rows twice (12 sts)

Dec 1 st at each end of next 3 rows (6 sts)

Cast off, taking 2 sts tog at each end of row at same time

Inside Arms

Work as for outside arms but start with the contrast colour (for paw pads) and change to main colour from **

Legs

make 2

With main colour cast on 32 sts

Starting with a K row, St st 4 rows

ROW 5—Dec 1 st at each end of row and following alt row (28 sts)

ROW 8—P

Cast off 6 sts at beg of next 2 rows

ROW 11—Inc 1 st at each end of row and every 4 th row until 24 sts

St st 6 rows

ROW 30—P2 tog, P8, P2 tog twice, P8, P2 tog

ROW 31—K

ROW 32—P2 tog, P6, P2 tog twice, P6,

P2 tog
Cast off remaining 16 sts, knitting 2 sts tog at each end of row at same time.

Soles
make 2

With contrast colour, cast on 4 sts
Starting with a K row, Inc 1 st at each end of every row until 10 sts
St st 13 rows
Dec 1 st at each end of row and following alt row (6 sts)
Dec 1 st at each end of row (4 sts)
K2 tog twice, pass 1 st over the other and finish off.

To make up

Press all the pieces on the purl side with a warm iron, especially at the edges where they tend to curl in. This will make sewing up the bear easier.

Head and Body and Limbs

With K sides together make up and stuff the head, body, arms and legs following the instructions for *Annie & George* (page 20).

Ears

Sew in and trim off the shorter cast on thread. Thread the longer thread onto the needle; weave it in along the edge of the ear down to the corner and pull slightly to give a nice rounded shape. Take a couple of sts to anchor the thread and use the rest to sew the ears to the head. Pin in position first, about ½ inch (1cm) in from the back of the head and about halfway across the head gusset seam. This is only a guide; you may like to experiment with the ear positions before sewing them on.

Eyes

If you are giving this bear to a child, use black embroidery thread and work a few tiny stitches for each eye.

As a collector's bear or mascot for an adult, you can use small black beads for the eyes. See General Instructions on page 13 for adding the eyes.

Nose and Mouth

Use three strands of black or dark brown embroidery thread to sew a nose and your choice of mouth. I think a big smile looks best on this bear!

Claws

With three strands of black or brown embroidery thread, make three claws on all four paws.

See General Instructions on page 13 sewing claws and thread-jointing your bear.

Overalls

Legs
make 2

With colour of choice, cast on 34 sts
G. st 2 rows (both rows K)
Starting with a K row, st st 16 rows

To shape crotch

Cast off 2 sts at the beg of the next 2 rows
St st a further 24 rows
NEXT ROW: (K6, K2 tog) 3 times, K6 (27 sts)
P 1 row
G. st 2 rows
Cast off

Bib
make 1

Cast on 20 sts
K1 row
ROW 2—K2, P to last 2 sts, K2
ROW 3—K
ROW 4—K2, P2 tog, P to last 4 sts, P2 tog, K2
Repeat the last 4 rows 3 times (12 sts)
G. st 3 rows
Cast off

Pockets
make 2

Cast on 10 sts
Starting with a K row, St st 9 rows
K 1 row
Cast off

Straps
make 2

Cast on 4 sts
Working in G. st, K until straps measure 4 inches (9cm)
Cast off

To make up overalls

With right sides together, fold each leg in half lengthways and sew up leg seam (shortest length of work is the legs).

Turn one leg right way out and fit this one inside the other. Sew up crotch seam and turn right side out.

Sew bib to front waistband of trousers. Sew on the two pockets. Sew one edge of each strap to the back of the overalls, about ½ inch (1cm) either side of the crotch seam, cross straps over at the back and sew the other end to the top of the bib at the front, overlapping ½ inch (1cm). Sew a button on the end of each strap (they will not undo). Dress bear and turn up bottom of trousers about ½ inch (1cm).

Robert

This cute little bear would be a great gift for an adult or for a slightly older child—he has the air of a wise old professor. He and his vest are knitted throughout in garter stitch. The advantage of this is that although strictly speaking, there is a right and wrong side of work, it doesn't really matter when all the edges are sewn together.

Materials

- Approx **4oz worsted (100g D/K) yarn** in the colour of your choice for bear
- Approx **1oz worsted (30g D/K) yarn** in contrasting colour for pads
- Approx **1oz worsted (30g D/K) yarn** in the colour of your choice for vest (waistcoat)
- A pair of **US 3 (3mm) knitting needles**
- Approx **3oz (90g) polyester stuffing**
- 1 pair ½ inch (10mm) **safety eyes**
- **4 pairs 1½ inch (35mm) joints** (optional) or **4 coat buttons** for joints (optional, not for children)
- **Black or brown embroidery thread or yarn** for nose, mouth and claws
- **2 small press fasteners** and buttons for vest

Height

Approximately 13¾ inches (35cm).

Robert can also be made in fingering (4-ply) yarn, using US 2 (2¾mm) needles. This will make him approximately 12 inches (30cm) high. Safety eyes size ¼ inch (7.5mm) in size are the most appropriate for the smaller bear.

As this bear is made using only G. st, both sides of the body, head, outside arms and legs are made the same, (one inside arm needs an extra row of contrast to reverse the 'joining line'). The disadvantage of G. st is that it is quite difficult to see which row you have increased or decreased in, so a row counter is a necessity, unless you are sure you will not get disturbed or lose your place.

Head

make 2

With main colour, cast on 12 sts and K 2 rows
Inc 1 st at each end of next and following 4 th row (16 sts)
K 1 row
NEXT ROW—Inc 1 st at beg of row
NEXT ROW—Inc 1 st at end of row
Rep the last 2 rows twice, then inc 1 st at beg of row once more (23 sts)
K 11 rows (ending at shaped edge)

To shape nose

Cast off 2 sts at beg of row and following 3 alt rows (15 sts)
NEXT ROW—Dec 1 st at beg of row
Dec 1 st at each end of next 4 rows
Cast off remaining 6 sts, knitting 2 sts tog at each end of row at the same time

Head Gusset

make 1

Starting at back neck edge
With main colour, cast on 5 sts and K 5 rows
Inc 1 st at each end of row and every 6th row until 15 sts
Knit 14 rows straight

To shape nose

Dec 1 st at each end of next and every following 4 th row until 7 st remain
K 10 rows straight
Dec 1 st at each end of next and following alt row
Cast off last 3 sts

Ears

make 2

(or 4 if double thickness ears required)
Cast on 11 sts and K 4 rows
Dec 1 st at each end of row and following 2 alt rows (5 sts)
Cast off, knitting 2 sts tog at each end of row at the same time and leaving a long thread

Body
make 2

Starting at base, make a dart as follows:
*With main colour, cast on 2 sts
Inc 1 st then at each end of next and every alt row until 12 sts
K 1 row **
Leave sts on a holder for now (or at back of needle) and make another piece the same by repeating from * to **
NEXT ROW—Inc 1 st at beg of row, knit to end and then across sts on holder, inc 1 st at end of row
K 1 row
NEXT ROW—Inc 1 st at each end of row (28 sts)
K 4 rows straight

To shape front
Inc 1 st at beg of row and following 4 th row (30 sts), mark the beginning of this row in some way to show which is the front edge, (I use a tiny safety pin)
K 14 rows straight, finishing at back edge

To shape back
NEXT ROW—Dec 1 st at beg of row (29 sts)
K 8 rows straight, finishing at front edge
Dec 1 st at beg of next row and every following 6 th row until 25 sts remain, finishing at back edge.
NEXT ROW—Dec 1 st at beg of row (24 sts)
K 5 rows straight

To make a shoulder dart
NEXT ROW—K2 tog, K10, turn and work on these sts for now *
K 1 row
Dec 1 st at each end of row and each following alt row until 3 sts
Cast off and break yarn
Rejoin yarn to remaining sts, starting at inside of dart, K to last 2 sts, K2 tog
Finish off second piece by repeating from * to end
Mark the last few sts with coloured thread to easily identify top of work when sewing up

Outside Arms
make 2

With main colour, cast on 4 sts
Inc 1 st at each end of next and every following 4 th row until 10 sts *

To shape paw
K 3 rows
NEXT ROW—Inc 1 st at beg of row and Dec 1 st at end of row
Rep the last 4 rows 3 times **
K 9 rows straight, finishing at back edge of arm
Inc 1 st at beg of next and following 10 th row (12 sts)
K 21 rows straight
Dec 1 st at each end of next and following 4 th row
K 1 row
Cast off remaining 8 sts, knitting 2 tog at each end of row at the same time

Left Inside Arm
In contrast colour, work as outside arms to *

To shape paw
Work the 4 paw shaping rows 3 times, change to main colour and rep once more
Complete as for rest of outside arms from **

Right Inside Arm
In contrast yarn, work as for outside arms to *

To shape paw
Work the 4 paw shaping rows 3 times
Knit 1 row
Change to main colour and knit 2 rows
NEXT ROW—Inc 1 st at beg of row and Dec 1 st at end of row
Complete as for rest of outside arms from **

Legs
make 2

In main colour, cast on 40 sts and
K 4 rows
To shape toes
NEXT ROW—Dec 1 st at each end of row
K 3 rows
NEXT ROW—Dec 1 st at each end of row and following alt row (34 sts)
K 1 row
Cast off 2 sts at beg of next 6 rows, slipping the first st each time to give a smoother finish (22 sts)
K 1 row
Dec 1 st at each end of row
K 2 rows
To shape legs
Inc 1 st at each end of row and every 12 th row until 26 sts
K 10 rows straight

NEXT ROW—K2 tog, K9, K2 tog twice, K9, K2 tog
K 1 row
NEXT ROW—K2 tog, K7, K2 tog twice, K7, K2 tog
Knit 1 row
NEXT ROW—K2 tog, K5, K2 tog twice, K5, K2 tog
K 1 row
NEXT ROW—K2 tog, K3, K2 tog twice, K3, K2 tog
Cast off remaining 10 sts

Soles
make 2
In contrast colour, cast on 4 sts
Inc 1 st at each end of row and following alt row (8 sts)
K 22 rows straight

Dec 1 st at each end of row and following alt row
Cast off remaining 4 sts

To make up
Do not press. Use an oversew st for sewing up the seams, keeping the sts small and close together.

Head
Sew the two head pieces together from the nose to the bottom of the neck (a–b). Pin, adjust and sew the head gusset to both sides of the head from the nose to the back of the head. When you are inserting safety eyes, it's a good idea to stuff the head roughly for now while you decide exactly where to place the eyes. Once you

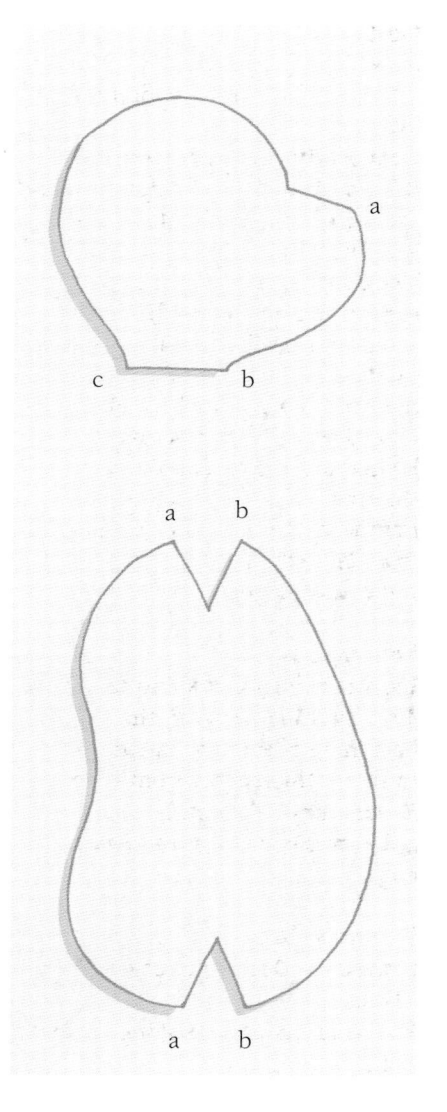

Body and head shapes: join (a) to (b) to sew up body darts.

have got a reasonable shape, push the shank of each eye carefully through the sts where you think they would look best (approximately halfway between the nose and the top of the head, on or near the seam line). When you are happy with the position, remove them one at a time, marking the spot with a couple of sts of contrast colour. Remove the stuffing again and fix in the eyes (try not to push the back washer too tightly all the way home or you'll squash the sts around the eyes). Stuff the head properly this time, carefully moulding into shape. Do not close the opening.

Body

Sew up the two darts in each body piece (joining "a" to "b" on the diagram on page 29), making sure the neat sides correspond with both sides of the body. To make this easier I usually sew a couple of inches of the front seam first, lay it out flat, then pin all four darts before sewing. Match up, pin and sew the body together, leaving a small gap at the centre back for stuffing. Stuff carefully, again moulding into shape, then close the gap in the back using ladderstitch.

Sew the head to the body all the way around the neck edge, adding a bit more stuffing as you go to make the neck firm.

Ears

If you want double thickness ears, sew two pieces together around the curved edges, leaving the bottom edge open. Turn out and oversew closed.

For single thickness ears, sew in and trim off the shorter cast on thread. Thread the long cast off thread at the top of the ears onto your needle. Weave this thread through the sts at the edge of one side of the ear down to the base, and pull slightly to "round off" the ear, then take a couple of sts to anchor the thread. Pin and sew the ears to the bear's head about 1 inch (2cm) in from the back of the head and with the head gusset seam running through the middle of the bottom of the ear, (this is only a guide, you may like to experiment with ear positions before sewing them on).

Nose and Mouth

Using black or brown embroidery thread or yarn, satin st your choice of nose, with 2 or 3 sts for the mouth.

Legs

Fold each leg in half lengthways, pin and sew, leaving the bottom edges open and a small gap at the front for turning and stuffing. Pin, adjust, and sew the soles to the feet. Turn out and stuff carefully, using small amounts of stuffing at a time. Check that each leg matches the other in size, then sew up the gap in the seams, using ladderstitch.

Arms

Match the pairs of arms together, pin and sew, leaving a small gap for turning and stuffing as for the legs. Turn out and stuff carefully, check they match in size and then close gap.

Use black or brown embroidery thread to make three or four small claws on each paw if required.

Attaching Arms and Legs

There are a number of different ways of attaching the arms and legs. You could either thread-joint them, use large matching buttons (which can look very attractive but are not suitable for children), or use plastic safety joints as in a fabric bear.

To thread-joint your bear—see General Instructions on page 13.

Using Buttons for 'Joints'

This is quite easy to do, very similar to thread jointing, except buttons are added as you come to the outside of each limb. Keep the entry and exit holes close together to give maximum movement.

Safety Joints

These joints are used on the inside of the limbs. They aren't difficult to attach but may not be easy to buy, and are not strictly necessary for this bear. It is, of course, an option for those that have them and want to use them.

Vest (waistcoat)
Left Front

In colour of choice, cast on 2 sts
Inc 1 st at each end of next and every following alt row until 20 sts*
Mark the beginning of this row (which will now be the side edge) with a coloured thread
K straight until work measures

3 inches (8cm) or 2½ inches (6cm) for a bear made using fingering-weight (4-ply) yarn from the beginning, finishing at the side edge.

To shape armholes

Cast off 5 sts at beg of next row
K 1 row
NEXT ROW—K1, K2 tog, K to last 3 sts, K2 tog, K1

To shape front edge

K 3 rows
NEXT ROW—K to last 3 sts, K2 tog, K1
Rep the last 4 rows until 6 sts remain
K a further 6 rows straight. Cast off

Right Front

Work as for left front to *
K 1 row
Mark the beginning of this row as the side edge and complete as for left front

Back

Cast on 36 sts and work straight until work measures the same as side edges of fronts up to the armhole shaping.

To shape armholes

Cast off 5 sts at beg of next 2 rows
NEXT ROW—K1, K2 tog, K to last 3 sts, K2 tog, K1
Continue straight until back measures the same as fronts to top of shoulders
Cast off

To make up

Sew up shoulder seams. Sew press fasteners to front edges of vest and buttons to the outside over the top of the fasteners (there are no button holes).

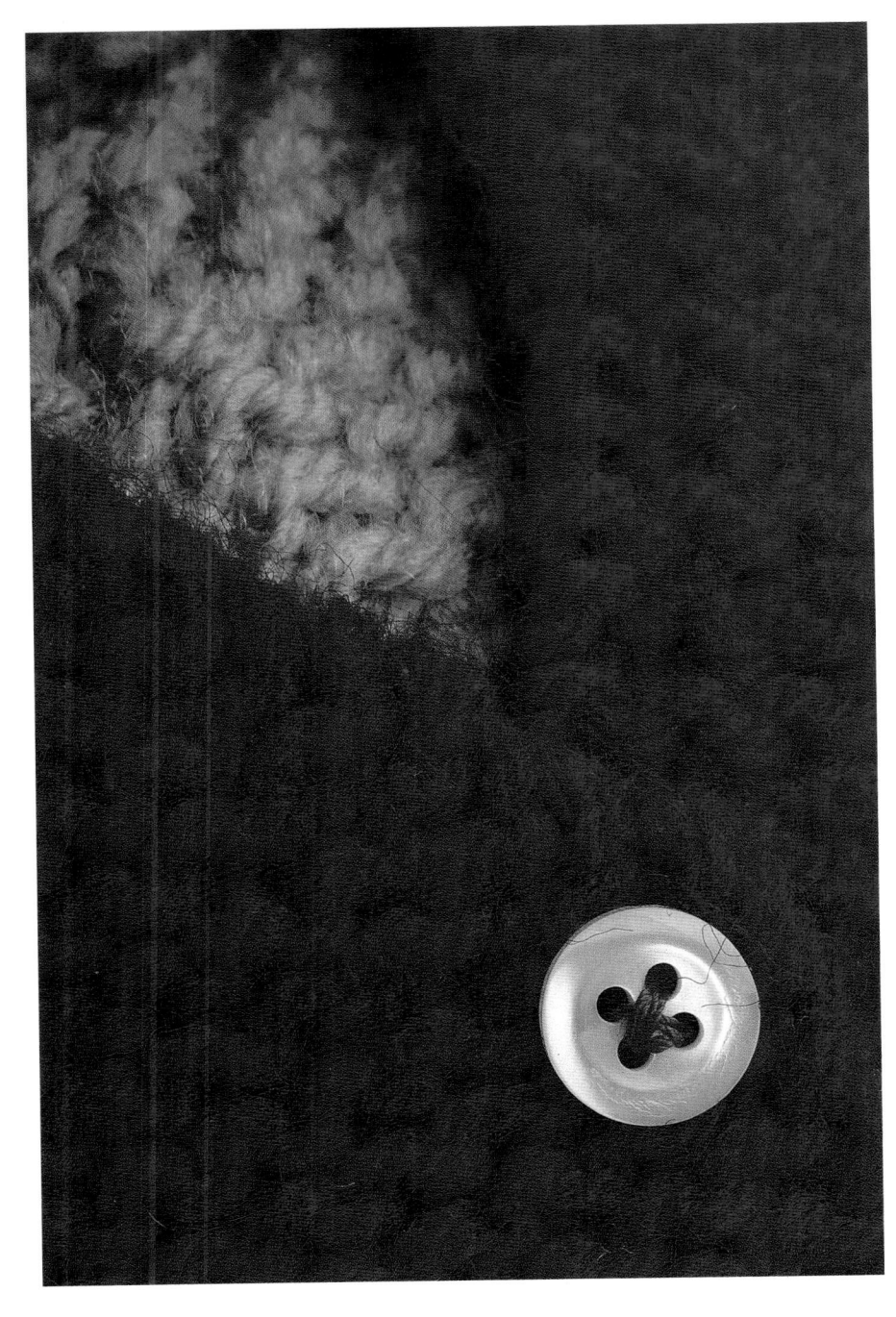

Beginner's Bears

These little teddies are very easy to make from quite small amounts of yarn, and you can use almost any colour or type of yarn you like. They are made from five rectangles, the ears are formed by tying two corners of the head. You can make lots of different bears just by knitting larger or smaller rectangles and using different types of yarn.

Materials needed for each bear

- **1oz worsted (30g D/K) yarn**
- **A pair of US 3 (3mm) knitting needles**
- **A tapestry or wool needle** for sewing up the bears
- **A sewing needle and cotton** for the lacy shawl (if required)
- **Polyester stuffing**
- **Brown or black embroidery thread** or yarn to sew the nose and mouth
- **2 small beads** for the eyes.
- **Extra strong thread** to sew on the bead eyes
- **4 matching buttons** for joints (optional)
- **Lace and ribbon** as required

The bears shown are knitted in recycled yarn.

Garter stitch bear

Body and Head
make 1

The body and head are both made out of one piece of knitting.
Cast on 30 sts and work in G. st until your work measures 5 inches (13cm) from the beginning.
Cast off

Arms
make 2

Cast on 10 sts and K until your work measures 2 inches (5cm) from the beginning.
Cast off

Legs
make 2

Cast on 12 sts and K until your work measures 2½ inches (6cm) from the beginning.
Cast off

To make up

You should now have 5 oblong pieces of knitting ready to sew up and stuff.

Head and Body

Thread a length of yarn onto your tapestry needle and tie a knot at the end. Fold your work in half lengthways (with the two sides together). Using an oversew st, sew up one short edge and the long edge, leaving one edge open for now, take a couple of sts to finish off and cut your thread. Turn the other way out so that you have neat seams on the outside. The closed end will be the head.

To Shape the Ears

At the top of the head, tie a length of yarn around each corner (see diagram "a" on page 34), a little way in, and pull up tightly (you might have to have a couple of tries until you are happy with the size of the ears).

Stuff firmly and evenly. When you think you have put enough stuffing in, thread and knot another piece of yarn and make a running st around the edges of the open end, then pull

up the sts to close. This will be teddy's bottom.

To shape the head

Tie a length of yarn about two thirds of the way up from the bottom (indicated in diagram "a" by dotted line), pull up tightly and tie a knot, thread the loose ends onto your needle and sink them into the body somewhere out of sight.

To shape the muzzle

Following diagram "b", right, make a running st around the front of the head and then pull up, not too tightly, to form the muzzle. Fasten off with a couple of sts.

Arms and Legs

Sew up the arms and legs in the same way as the body and head piece, leaving one end open for turning and stuffing. Turn out and stuff carefully and before sewing up the last edges, check that both the legs are the same size as each other. Then do the same with the arms.

Loose Threads

When you have knitted and sewn up all the pieces, you will need to tidy up all the loose threads. The best way to do this is to sew them into the inside of the stuffed bear parts out of sight. Trim and thread each loose end onto your tapestry needle, push the needle and thread into the bear and bring it out a bit further away, pull the thread tightly and snip it off close to your knitting. You will see that the end springs back into the bear out of sight.

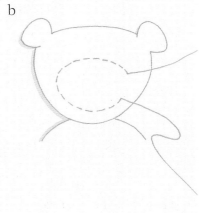

With these bears the ears can be formed by tying yarn around the corners of the head (a). The muzzle is similarly shaped (b).

To Attach the Arms and Legs using buttons

Thread a long length of extra strong thread or yarn onto your needle and following the diagram opposite, push your needle into the place where your first arm is going to be, through the body and out to where the second arm is to be joined on. Go through that arm, out the other side and through a hole of one of your buttons, then back in again through the other button hole. Go back into the body, out the other side and do exactly the same with the other arm, you should now be back to where you started. It's a good idea to repeat this process a couple of times for extra strength. Pull the threads quite tightly and tie them with a couple of knots. Rethread and sink the ends into the body out of sight.

The legs of the bear are joined on in the same way.

Eyes

Little black beads make very nice eyes and are quite easy to sew on.

Thread a bead with a long length of extra strong black thread, then thread both ends onto your tapestry needle. Push your needle down into the place where the first eye is to be and bring it out at the back of your bears neck, pull the threads through and leave them hanging there for a moment. Do the same with the second eye, bringing your needle out very close to the first threads. Now tie both the sets of threads together, pulling until the eyes sink a little way into the head. Trim and sink the ends

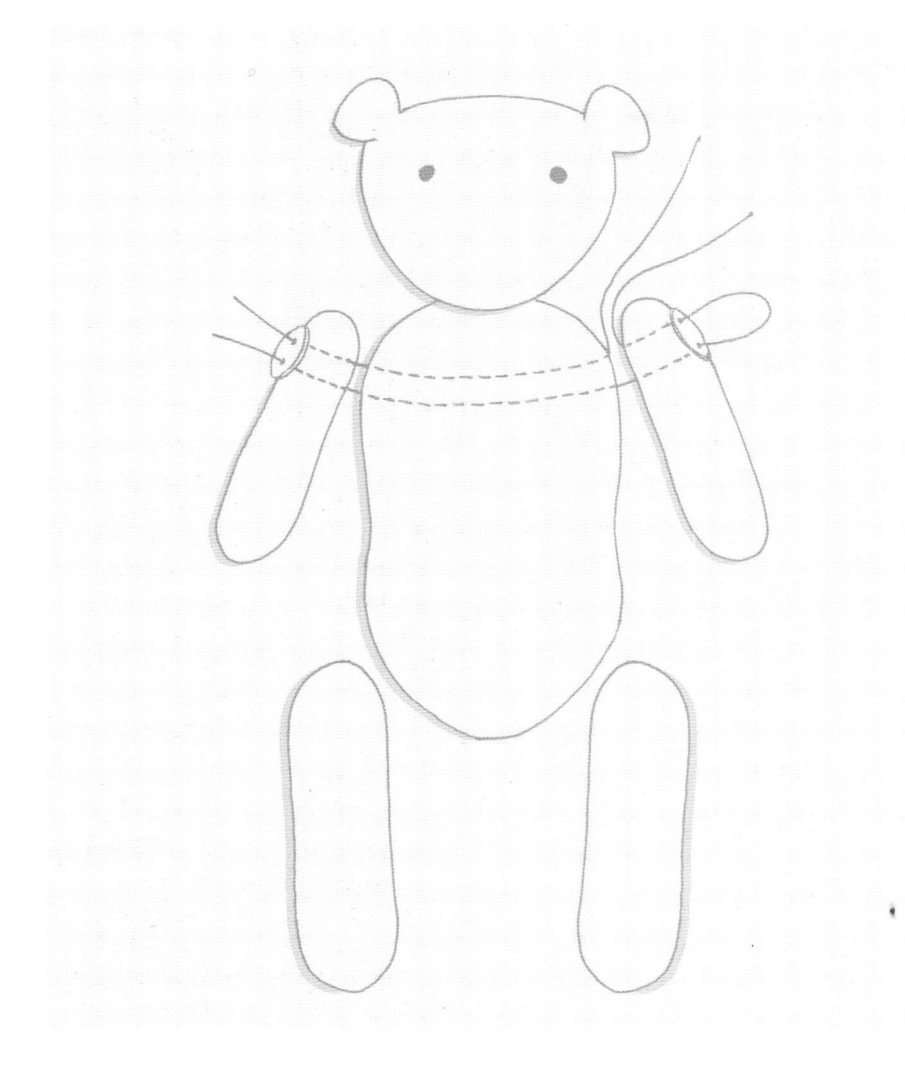

Stocking stitch bear

Start all the pieces with a K row and finish them with a P row. Cast off using the K stitch.

Body and Head
make 1

Cast on 30 sts and continue until your knitting measures 4½ inches (11cm) from the beginning.
Cast off

Legs
make 2

Cast on 12 sts and continue until your work measures 1¾ inches (4½cm).
Cast off

Arms
make 2

Cast on 10 sts and continue until your work measures 2 inches (5cm) .
Cast off

To make up

Make up all the pieces and shape the head following the instructions for the G. st bear. Don't forget to tie the corners to make the ears before stuffing the head and body. After stuffing, oversew the bottom edges closed but do not gather.

When stuffing the arms and legs, put only a little bit of stuffing at the tops ends or teddy will not be able to sit very well and his arms will stick out too much.

Sew the tops of the legs to the bottom of the body. Then hold each arm against the body and sew the top a little way down from the neck with

into the body out of sight. If the beads disappear between the stitches of your knitting, then you will need to sink the two ends of the thread separately, with one or two stitches between them.

If you haven't got any beads you can embroider some eyes by making some tiny little stitches on top of each other.

Nose and Mouth

Use your embroidery thread or brown or black yarn to stitch a nose and mouth (as described on page 14).

your sewing line running from the front to the back of the body as shown on the diagram below. You could pin them in place first to see how they look. If the arms do stick up a bit, sew an extra couple of sts either side just down from the top.

For the shawl, I used a small piece of lace edging, sewn together at the front and with a little bow sewn on. A little pearl necklace would also look nice. Most sewing and craftstores sell little pots of beads, lace, pretty ribbon, and anything else you may wish to finish off your bears with.

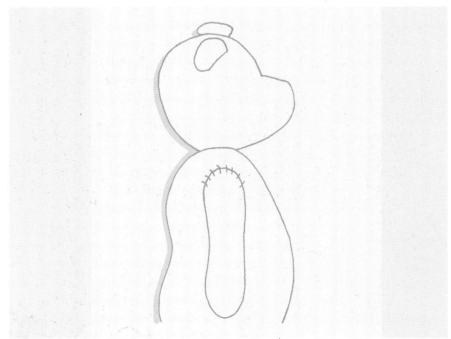

Adding a few stitches around the top of the bears' arms will help prevent them from sticking out.

Thomas

This bear is very sweetly dressed and is ready to go on an adventure in his jacket and jeans.
He would make a great little friend for an older child.

Materials
• Approx **1oz fingering (30g 4-ply) yarn** in the colour of your choice for the bear
• Approx **1oz fingering (30g 4-ply) yarn** in a contrasting shade for the paw pads
• Approx **1oz fingering (30g 4-ply) yarn** in three different colours for the clothes
• A pair of **US 2 (2¾mm) knitting needles** for bear and clothes
• Approx **1oz (30g) polyester stuffing**
• A **tapestry or wool needle** for sewing up bear
• **Black or brown embroidery thread** for eyes, nose, mouth and claws
• **3 small buttons** for jacket (plus press fasteners if required)
• **Small crochet hook** for scarf fringe if required

The bear shown is knitted in Paton Diploma Gold 4-ply Soft Camel (4292) with jacket in Navy (4287), trousers in Denim (4136) and scarf and jumper in Cherry (4239).
Alternative yarns: Jaeger Matchmaker Merino 4-ply in shades Soft Camel (718), Mid Navy (728), Baltic Blue (740), Peony (697).

Height
Approximately 9½ inches (24cm).

Work in St st throughout and start all pieces with a K row unless otherwise stated.

Head and Body
Side A
With main colour, cast on 9 sts.
Inc 1 st at each end of every row until 19 sts
ROW 6—P
ROW 7—(K3, Inc 1) 4 times, K3 (23 sts)
St st 23 rows **
ROW 31—Dec 1 st at beg of row and every alt row until 18 sts
ROW 40—P
ROW 41—Dec 1 st at each end of row and 2 following alt rows (12 sts)
ROW 46—P

To shape head
ROW 47—Inc 1 st at each end of row (14 sts)
ROW 48—Inc 1 st at end of row
ROW 49—Inc 1 st at beg of row
Repeat last 2 rows three times (22 sts)
St st 5 rows
ROW 61—Dec 1 st at end of row (21 sts)
ROW 62—P

To shape nose
ROW 63—Cast off 7 sts, K to last 2 sts, K2 tog

P 1 row
Dec 1 st at each end of next 3 rows
Cast off remaining 7 sts.

Head and body
Side B
Work as for head and body side A until **
ROW 31—Dec 1 st at end of row and every alt row until 18 sts
ROW 40—P
ROW 41—Dec 1 st at each end of row and 2 following alt rows (12 sts)
ROW 46—P

To shape head
ROW 47—Inc 1 st at each end of row (14 sts)
ROW 48—Inc 1 st at beg of row
ROW 49—Inc 1 st at end of row
Rep last 2 rows three times (22 sts)
St st 5 rows
ROW 61—Dec 1 st at beg of row (21 sts)
ROW 62—P

To shape nose
ROW 63 —K2 tog, K to last 7 sts, cast off 7 sts. Break yarn.
With P side facing, rejoin yarn to remaining sts, P 1 row
Dec 1 st at each end of next 3 rows
Cast off remaining 7 sts.

Head Gusset
Starting at nose

With main colour, cast on 4 sts
ROW 1—Inc 1 st at each end of row
and following alt row (8 sts)
St st 7 rows
ROW 11—Inc 1 st at each end of row
and 2 following alt rows (14 sts)
St st 13 rows
ROW 29—Dec 1 st at each end of row
and every following alt row until 4 sts
P 1 row
K2 tog twice
P2 tog and fasten off

Ears
make 4
With main colour, cast on 8 sts
Starting with a K row, St st 3 rows
Dec 1 st at each end of next 2 rows
Cast off

Arm
Outside left
make 1
Starting at paw
With main colour, cast on 5 sts
ROW 1—Inc 1 st at each end of row
and following alt row (9 sts)
ROW 4—P
ROW 5—Inc 1 st at beg of row and
following alt row (11 sts)
ROW 8—P
ROW 9—Inc 1 st at beg and dec 1 st
at end of row
ROW 10—P
Rep last 2 rows **
ROW 13—Dec 1 st at end of row
(10 sts)
St st 3 rows (ending on a P row)
ROW 17—Inc 1 st at beg of row
(11 sts)
St st 3 rows
ROW 21—Inc 1 st at beg of row

(12 sts)
St st 15 rows (ending on a P row)
ROW 37—Dec 1 st at each end of row
and following alt row (8 sts)
ROW 40—Cast off

Arm
Outside right
make 1
With main colour, cast on 5 sts
ROW 1—Inc 1 st at each end of row
and following alt row (9 sts)
ROW 4—P
ROW 5—Inc 1 st at end of row and
following alt row (11 sts)
ROW 8—P
ROW 9—Dec 1 st at beg and Inc 1 st at
end of row
ROW 10—P
Rep last 2 rows **
ROW 13—Dec 1 st at beg of row (10 sts)
St st 3 rows (ending on a P row)
ROW 17—Inc 1 st at end of row
(11 sts)
St st 3 rows
ROW 21—Inc 1 st at end of row
(12 sts)
St st 15 rows
ROW 37—Dec 1 st at each end of row
and following alt row (8 sts)
ROW 40—Cast off

Inside Arms
Work a pair of arms as for outside
arms but use contrast colour up to **
then change to main colour.

Legs
make 2
With main colour, cast on 32 sts
St st 6 rows
ROW 7—Dec 1 st at each end of row

and following alt row (28 sts)
Cast off 4 sts at beg of next 2 rows
ROW 12—P
ROW 13—Inc 1 st at each end of row
St st 6 rows
Rep last 7 rows once (24 sts)
ROW 27—Inc 1 st at each end of row
(26 sts)
St st 5 rows
ROW 33—K2 tog, K9, K2 tog twice,
K9, K2 tog (22 sts)
ROW 34—P
ROW 35—K2 tog, K7, K2 tog twice,
K7, K2 tog (18 sts)
Cast off in P

Soles
make 2
With contrast colour, cast on 5 sts
Inc 1 st at each end of row and
following alt row (9 sts)
St st 12 rows
Dec 1 st at each end of row and
following alt row (5 sts)
Cast off

To make up
Darn in and snip off loose threads.
Press all the pieces on the purl side
with a warm iron, especially at the
edges where they tend to curl in, then
match all pieces K sides together to
sew up.

Head and Body
With K sides together make up
following the instructions for
Annie & George on pages 16–21.

Ears
With right sides together, sew ear
pieces together in pairs around

curved edges using an oversew st, leaving bottom edges open. Turn right side out and oversew bottom edges together (do not stuff). Pin and sew ears to bear's head about ¾ inch (1cm) in from the back of the head and with the head gusset seam running through the middle of the bottom of the ear, (this is only a guide, you may like to experiment with ear positions before sewing them on).

Eyes

Make two or three small sts on top of each other with black or brown embroidery thread in each eye position. One tiny st in white thread over the top will bring the eyes to life.

Nose and Mouth

Using black or brown embroidery thread, sew a triangle in satin st for the nose and work 3 little sts for the mouth.

Legs

Fold each leg in half lengthways (K sides together), pin and sew, leaving the bottom edges open and a small gap at the front for turning and stuffing. Pin, adjust, and sew the soles to the feet. Turn out and stuff carefully, using small amounts of stuffing at a time. Check that each leg matches the other in size, then sew up the gap in the seams, using ladder st.

Arms

Match the pairs of arms (K sides together), pin and sew, leaving a small gap at the back for turning and stuffing. Turn out and stuff carefully, check they match in size and then close gap.

Claws

With black or brown embroidery thread or yarn, make 3 claws on all four paws as follows: Knot the end of a length of thread. Take the needle and thread into the paw, coming out at the beginning of the first claw and pulling the thread until the knotted end disappears into the paw. Make three "claws" and then pull the needle out further up the limb, push the needle back in exactly the same hole, come back out a bit further away, pull the thread to create some tension, snip off close to the surface and the thread should disappear into the bear.

To Attach Limbs

Using a double length of bear-coloured yarn, take a few sts from the inside of the tops of the arms and legs (about ½ inch or 2cm down) and go through the body to do the same with the corresponding limbs, pulling the yarn each time so that the limbs fit snugly into the body. Do this several times until you are happy that they are secure, especially if Thomas is going to have his clothes changed frequently. Try not to spread the sts out too much or there will not be much range of movement in the limbs.

Jacket

Work in G. st throughout (every row knit). Although strictly speaking, there is a right and wrong side of work with garter stitch, with this jacket it doesn't really matter so you do not have to worry about reverse shaping.

Use size US 2 (2¾mm) knitting needles throughout.

Back

make 1

Cast on 30 sts and K until work measures 1 inch (4 cm)

To shape armholes

Cast off 4 sts at beg of next 2 rows
Work straight for a further 2 inches (5cm)

To shape neck

NEXT ROW—K7, cast off 8 sts, K7
Working on first 7 sts:
*Dec 1 st at neck edge on next 2 rows (5 sts)
K 1 row
Cast off and break yarn
Rejoin yarn to remaining sts and rep from *

Fronts

make 2

Cast on 17 sts and K until work measures 1½ inches (4 cm)

To shape armhole

Cast off 4 sts at beg of row
Work straight until armhole measures 1½ inches (4 cm), ending at front edge

To shape neck

Cast off 4 sts at beg of row
Dec 1 st at neck edge on next row and every following alt row until 5 sts remain

K 2 rows
Cast off

Sleeves
make 2

Cast on 25 sts
K 5 rows
NEXT ROW—Inc 1 st at each end of row
Repeat the last 6 rows until there are
35 sts on the needle
Mark each end of row with a
coloured thread
Work a further 6 rows
Cast off

Hood
make 1

Cast on 60 sts and K 4 rows
Dec 1 st at each end of next and
every following alt row until 40 sts
Cast off 14 sts at beg of next 2 rows
and mark beg of each row
Continue straight on remaining 12 sts
for 22 rows
Cast off and mark each end of row
Sew up back panel by matching the
markers each side and joining the 14
st cast off edges to the 22 row ends.

To make up

Use an oversew st to join all seams.
Sew up shoulder seams and then lay
your work out flat.

To set in sleeves

Match top of sleeves to row ends of
front and back armholes, with centre
of sleeve top matching shoulder seam
and markers matching front and back
side edges, (see diagram, right).
Pin and sew
Sew up side seams

To sew on hood

Starting and finishing 4 sts in at either
side of front edge, pin and sew
shaped edges of hood to neck edge of
jacket (right sides tog). It will be
easier if you match centre of hood
base to centre of back neck edge first,
then adjust to fit.

To finish, sew on three matching
beads or small buttons, with press
fasteners on the inside and adjacent
side of front if you want to fasten
the jacket.

Scarf

With size US 2 (2¾mm) needles, cast
on 6 sts and work in G. st until
required length (approx. 10 inches or
25cm).
Cast off

To make fringe

Cut 12 lengths of yarn about 3½
inches (8cm) long. Fold a length in
half, insert your crochet hook through
a stitch at the very edge of the scarf
and draw the centre of the piece of
yarn through forming a loop. Draw
the 2 ends of the yarn through the
loop and gently pull to form a knot.
Continue in this way along each edge
of the scarf then trim evenly to required
length. For bigger scarves, increase the
amount of threads per loop.

Woolly Hat

With size US 2 (2¾mm) knitting
needles, cast on 48 sts
Work 3 cm in K1, P1 rib.

*Attaching jacket sleeves and making the
fringe for the scarf.*

Starting with a k row, St st a further 2 inches (4cm).

To shape top
ROW 1—K2 tog to end (24 sts)
ROW 2—P
Repeat the last 2 rows twice (6 sts)
Break yarn and thread it through the remaining sts, draw up tightly and fasten off. Sew up back seam.

Pompom
To make a quick small pompom, wrap yarn around 2 fingers and your thumb about 24 times. Slip the loops from your fingers and tie a length of yarn tightly around the middle. Cut

Shawl neck sweater

I adapted this sweater from an old children's pattern I found in a charity shop. It is exactly like one my mother knitted for my three brothers and I when we were children. They were all from the same pattern but theirs were blue and mine was pink. My mother says that the reason they were all the same was because they were quick and easy to make and nice and warm in the winter, (especially as there was no central heating then). They certainly kept our necks warm!

through the loops and trim the tufts into a nice round shape.

It was quite nostalgic finding this design and I think Thomas looks very smart in it.

Use size US 2 (2¾mm) knitting needles throughout.

Front
Cast on 32 sts
Work 3 rows single rib
Starting with a k row, St st until work measures 2 inches (5cm), ending on a P row.
NEXT ROW—K11, turn, leaving remaining 21 sts on a holder for now
Working on these sts only for now, continue in St st until work measures 3¾ inches (9cm) from beginning
Cast off and break yarn.
With P side facing, replace the first 11 of the 21 sts from the holder onto your needle. Turn, rejoin yarn and complete to match the first side.
Cast off

Back
Cast on 32 sts
Work 3 rows single rib
Starting with a K row, work in St st until back measures 3¾ inches (9cm) from beginning
Cast off

There are two ways to make the sleeves, either in the conventional way (described under "A" below) and sewing on afterwards, or you can pick up the sts from the shoulder and then work down to the wrist (described under "B" below).

Sleeves

make 2

(A)

Cast on 28 sts and rib 4 rows
St st 4 rows
Inc 1 st at each end of row and every following 4 th row until 34 sts
St st 3 more rows.
Cast off loosely.

Or (B)

Join shoulder seams of jumper then lay your work out flat
With right side facing, pick up and K 34 sts evenly along top of shoulder (starting and finishing 2 inches (5cm) before and after seam line)
Starting with a K row, St st 3 rows
Dec 1 st at each end of next and every following 4 th row until 28 sts
St st 4 rows
Rib 4 rows
Cast off loosely in rib.

Collar

With right side facing, place 10 sts from holder onto needle and rejoin yarn.
Inc 1, rib to last st, Inc 1 (12 sts)
Continue straight in rib until collar measures 6 inches (15 cm).
Cast off loosely in rib.

To make up

Press all the pieces if necessary. If the sleeves have been made separately, fold to find the centre top and mark with a pin. With right sides together, pin and sew the sleeves to the shoulders. Sew up side seams. Pin, adjust to fit and sew one side of the row ends of the collar in place around the neck and the cast off edge tucked inside and sewn behind the beginning of the collar.

Jeans

make 2 pieces

Starting at bottom of leg
With size US 2 (2¾mm) needles, cast on 35 sts and G. st 2 rows
Starting with a K row, St st 16 rows
Shape crotch
Cast off 2 sts at beginning of next 2 rows
St st a further 20 rows
NEXT ROW—(K2, K2 tog) to last 3 sts, K3
G. st 3 rows
Cast off.

Pockets (optional)

make 2

Cast on 10 sts and St st 9 rows
K 1 row
Cast off.

To make up

With right sides together, fold each leg in half lengthways and sew up leg seam (shortest length of work is the legs). Turn one leg right way out and fit this one inside the other. Sew up crotch seam and turn right side out. Sew on the 2 pockets.

Sporty Thomas (pattern opposite) has a football shirt and scarf.

Sporty Thomas

This bear is made as for Thomas but his outfit has been adapted for different types of sports. It is quite easy to add or take away stripes and change rib colours. Plus there is an easy-to-use chart for knitting the number of your choice into his sports shirt.

Materials
- Approx **1oz fingering (30g 4-ply) yarn** in colours of choice
- **Size 2 (2¾mm) knitting needles** for shirt and shorts
- **Size 1 (2¼mm) knitting needles** for hat and scarf
- **Safety pin** (to use as st holder)

Sporty Thomas's shirt and shorts shown here are knitted in Jaeger Matchmaker fingering weight (4-ply) in Peony (697) and White (661).
NB. When working with two colours, you must twist the yarns together whenever you change colour or a gap will form.

Shirt
Back
make 1
With size 1 (2¼mm) needles and white, cast on 30 sts and work 3 rows in single rib
Change to size 2 (2¾mm) needles and contrast and St st straight for 12 rows. Place a marker at each end of last row.

To shape armholes
Dec 1 st at each end of next 4 rows (22 sts)**

To knit number
Continuing in St st, follow the chart for your number of choice. Check the start position; for example, the number 7 will start on the 12th st. After completing the number, St st straight for a further 4 rows.

To shape shoulders
Cast off 5 sts at beg of next 2 rows (12 sts)
Change back to size 1 (2¼mm) needles and white, and work 3 rows in single rib, then cast off loosely.

Front
make 1
Work as for back to **
St st straight for 9 rows

To shape right side of neck
NEXT ROW—P8, turn and work on these sts for now
Dec 1 st at neck edge on next 3 rows (5 sts)
St st 4 rows
Cast off

To shape left side of neck
With wrong side facing, place next 6 sts on a safety pin, rejoin yarn and P to end
Dec 1 st at neck edge on next 3 rows
St st 3 rows
Cast off remaining 5 sts

Sleeves
make 2
With size 1 (2¼mm) needles and white, cast on 31 sts and work 2 rows in single rib
Change to size 2 (2¾mm) needles and contrast St st 3 rows
NEXT ROW—Inc 1 st at each end of row
St st 2 more rows and place markers at each end of last row.

To shape sleeve top
Dec 1 st at each end of next 5 rows (23 sts)
Cast off in P

To make up
Press pieces lightly if necessary.
With size 1 (2¼ mm) needles and white, knit front neck rib. With right side of work facing, pick up and K8 sts evenly along left side of neck, K across 6 sts on safety pin, then pick up and K8 sts along right side of neck. Work 3 rows single rib on these 22 sts, then cast off loosely.
Join front and back at shoulder seams (including rib) and side seams up to markers.
Join sleeve seams from wrist to markers. Sew sleeves K sides facing and turn right side out.

Shorts
make 2
With white, cast on 35 sts and K 1 row

To make stripe
NEXT ROW—K16 sts white, join in and

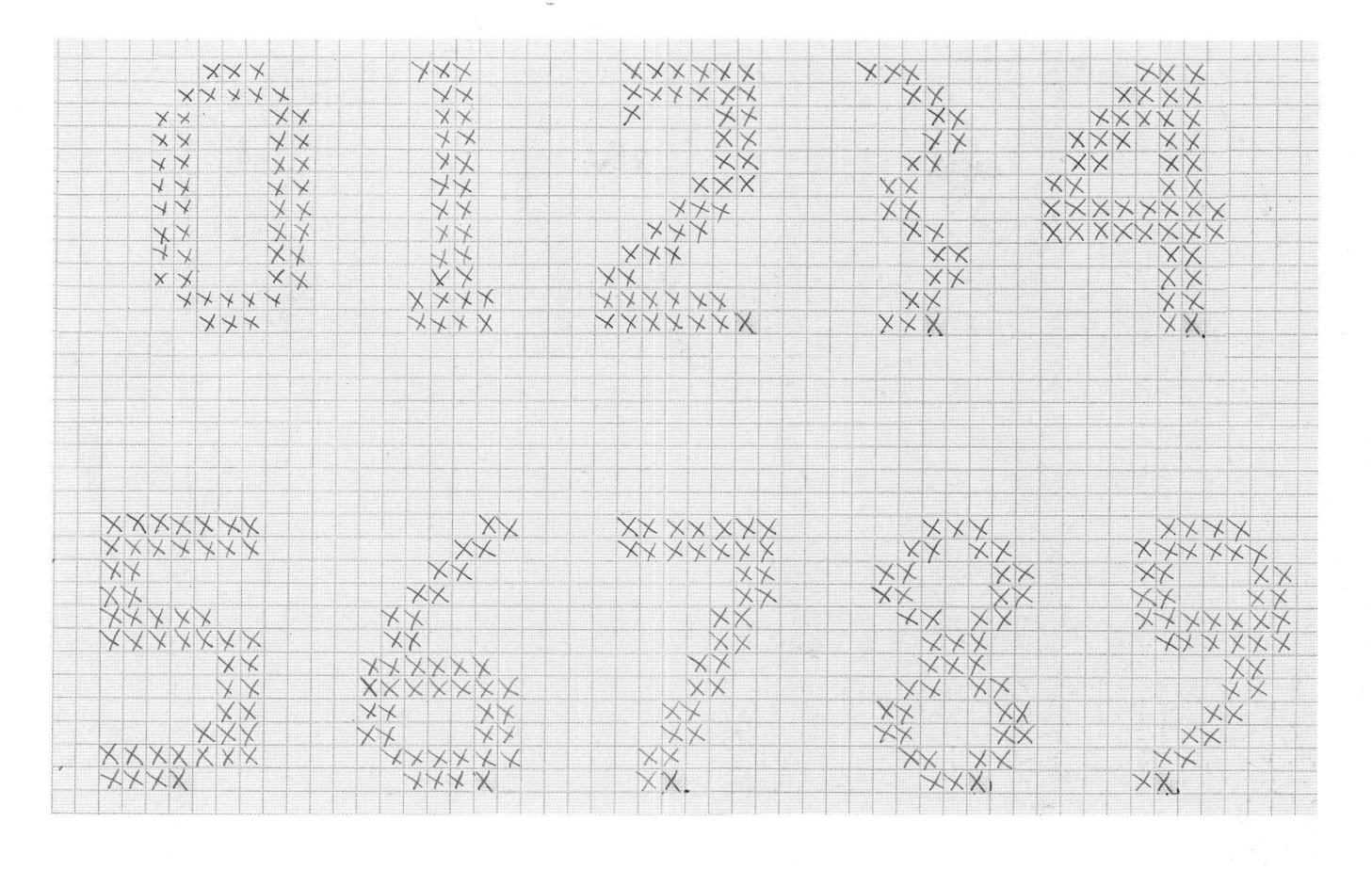

K 3 sts in contrast, K16 sts in white
NEXT ROW—P 16 white, 3 contrast,
16 white
Keep to the colours as set.
St st 2 more rows.

To shape crotch
Cast off 2 sts at beg of next 2 rows
(31 sts)
St st 20 rows straight
Break off contrast and continue in
white only
NEXT (DEC) ROW—(K2, K2 tog) to last
3 sts, K3 (24 sts)

G. st 3 rows
Cast off
Make up as for jeans on page 44.

Pull-on Hat
With size US 1 (2¼mm) needles and
main colour, work as for Thomas's
woolly hat but work in single rib only
and omit the pompom.

Scarf
The scarf can be a main colour
with white stripes or white with
contrast stripes.

With size 1 (2¼mm) needles and
main colour, cast on 10 sts and work
in single rib until the scarf measures
1¼ inches (3cm). Join in contrast and
work 2 rows, followed by 4 rows in
main colour. Rep until 3 contrast
stripes have been made. Continue
in main colour until scarf measures
8½ inches (22cm) (or length required).
Make 3 more contrast stripes, then
work 1¼ inches (3cm) in main
colour. Cast off. Fringe each end of
the scarf with contrast following
instructions given on page 42.

Catherine

Catherine is the largest bear in the book. She is designed and made up in the same way as a traditional, old-style bear with fully jointed arms and legs and a humped back.

Materials
- Approx 4 x 2oz worsted (4 x 50g D/K) yarn in colour of your choice for the bear
- Approx 3 x 2oz balls of fingering weight (50g 4-ply) cotton for dress
- A pair of US 3 (3mm) knitting needles for bear and dress
- A pair of US 2 (2¾ mm) knitting needles for neck and sleeve edging on dress and nose
- Approx 7oz (200g) polyester stuffing
- A tapestry or wool needle for sewing up bear
- ½ inch (13½mm) safety eyes
- Black embroidery thread or yarn for mouth and claws
- Black or charcoal yarn to knit nose
- 5 x 2–2½ inch (50–55mm) diameter plastic safety joints
- 2 small buttons for dress
- Stitch holder for dress

The bear shown here is knitted in Rowan Kid Classic D/K yarn in Wild (816) with the dress in Rowan 4-ply cotton White (113).

Height
Approximately 21 inches (53cm).

Catherine is knitted in St st throughout. Start all pieces with a K row unless otherwise stated. Where instructions are given to put markers, use a needle and length of differently coloured thread and take a couple of sts, this will make sewing up and placing eyes and joints much easier.

Body
side A
make 1

Cast on 6 sts
ROW 1—Inc in each st (12 sts)
ROW 2—P
ROW 3—Inc 1, K4, Inc in next 2 sts, K3, Inc 1, K1
ROW 4—P
ROW 5—Inc 1, K6, Inc in next 2 sts, K5, Inc 1, K1
ROW 6—P
ROW 7—Inc 1, K8, Inc in next 2 sts, K7, Inc 1, K1 (24 sts)
ROW 8—P
Continue in this way, inc 2 sts in middle of row and 1 st at each end of next row and every following alt row until 40 sts.
ROW 16—P
ROW 17—K19, Inc in next 2 sts, K19
ROW 18—P
ROW 19—Inc 1, K19, Inc in next 2 sts, K18, Inc 1, K1
ROW 20—P
ROW 21—K22, Inc in next 2 sts, K22
ROW 22—P
ROW 23—K23, Inc in next 2 sts, K23 (50 sts)
St st straight for 5 rows (ending on a P row).

To shape back
ROW 29—Dec 1 st at beg of row and each following 4 th row until 47 sts—mark beg of last row with a coloured marker.
St st 21 rows (ending on a P row).

To shape back hump
ROW 59—Inc 1 st at beg and Dec 1 st at end of row—mark beg of this row
St st 3 rows
ROW 63—Inc 1 st at beg of row
ROW 64—P
ROW 65—Dec 1 st at end of row (47 sts)
ROW 66—P
ROW 67—Inc 1 st at beg of row
St st 3 rows.

To shape front and shoulders
ROW 71—Dec 1 st at end of row and following 6 th row
ROW 78—P
ROW 79—K1, K2 tog, K20, K2 tog twice, K 19
ROW 80—P
ROW 81—K1, K2 tog, K18, K2 tog twice, K to end

ROW 82—P

ROW 83—K1, K2 tog, K16, K2 tog twice, K14, K2 tog, K1

ROW 84—P

ROW 85—K1, K2 tog, K14, K2 tog twice, K to end

ROW 86—P14, P2 tog twice, P15

ROW 87—K1, K2 tog, K11, K2 tog twice, K to end

ROW 88—P

ROW 89—K1, K2 tog, K9, K2 tog twice, K9, K2 tog, K1

ROW 90—P10, P2 tog twice, P10

ROW 91—K1, K2 tog, K6, K2 tog twice, K9

ROW 92—P

ROW 93—K1, K2 tog across row to last 2 sts, K2 (11 sts)

ROW 94—P2, P 2 sts tog across row to last st, P1

Cast off and mark with coloured thread to easily identify top of work when sewing up.

Body
Side B
make 1

Work as for side A until start of back shaping

ROW 29—Dec 1 st at end of row and each following 4 th row until 47 sts—mark end of last row with a coloured marker

St st 21 rows (ending on a P row)

To shape back hump

ROW 59—Dec 1 st at beg of row and Inc 1 st at end of row—mark end of this row

St st 3 rows

ROW 63—Inc 1 st at end of row

ROW 64—P

ROW 65—Dec 1 st at beg of row (47 sts)

ROW 66—P

ROW 67—Inc 1 st at end of row

St st 3 rows

To shape front and shoulders

ROW 71—Dec 1 st at beg of row and following 6 th row

ROW 78—P

ROW 79—K19, K2 tog twice, K20, K2 tog, K1

ROW 80—P

ROW 81—K18, K2 tog twice, K18, K2 tog, K1

ROW 82—P

ROW 83—K1, K2 tog, K14, K2 tog twice, K16, K2 tog, K1

ROW 84—P

ROW 85—K15, K2 tog twice, K14, K2 tog, K1 (33 sts)

ROW 86—P15, P2 tog twice, P14

ROW 87—K13, K2 tog twice, K11, K2 tog, K1

ROW 88—P

ROW 89—K1, K2 tog, K9, K2 tog twice, K9, K2 tog, K1

ROW 90—P10, P2 tog twice, P10

ROW 91—K9, K2 tog twice, K6, K2 tog, K1

ROW 92—P

ROW 93—K2, K2 tog across row, to last st, K1 (11 sts)

ROW 94—P2 tog to last 2 sts, P2

Cast off and mark with coloured thread

Head
Right side
make 1

Cast on 19 sts

ROW 1—K

ROW 2—Inc 1 st at end of row

St st 3 rows

ROW 6—Inc 1 st at each end of row

ROW 7—K

To shape chin

ROW 8—Inc 1 st at end of row

ROW 9—Inc 1 st at beg of row

Rep last 2 rows once (26 sts)

ROW 12—Inc 1 st at each end of row

Work 5 rows, increasing 1 st at shaped (chin) edge only on every row (33 sts)

ROW 18—Inc 1 st at each end of row

Continue to inc at shaped edge only in every row as before until 40 sts (ending on a K row)

St st 9 rows

To shape nose

ROW 33—Cast off 7 sts at beg of row

ROW 34—P to last 2 sts, P2 tog

ROW 35—Cast off 7 sts at beg of row, slipping the first st (25 sts)

ROW 36—P (mark the end of this row with a coloured thread)

Dec 1 st at each end of every row until 11 sts

Cast off, purling 2 sts tog at each end of row at same time.

Head
Left side
make 1

Cast on 19 sts

ROW 1—P

ROW 2—Inc 1 st at end of row

St st 3 rows

ROW 6—Inc 1 st at each end of row

ROW 7—P

To shape chin

ROW 8—Inc 1 st at end of row
ROW 9—Inc 1 st at beg of row
Rep last 2 rows once (26 sts)
ROW 12—Inc 1 st at each end of row
Work 5 rows, Inc 1 st at shaped
(chin) edge only in every row (33 sts)
ROW 18—Inc 1 st at each end of row
Continue to Inc at shaped edge on
every row as before until 40 sts
(ending on a P row)
St st 9 rows

To shape nose

ROW 33—Cast off 7 sts at beg of row
ROW 34—K to last 2 sts, K2 tog
ROW 35—Cast off 7 sts at beg of row,
slipping the first st (25 sts)
ROW 36—K (mark the end of this row
with a coloured thread)
Dec 1 st at each end of every row
until 11 sts
Cast off, knitting 2 sts tog at each end
of row at the same time.

Head Gusset

make 1

Cast on 4 sts Start with a K row
Inc 1 st at each end of row and every
4 th row until 24 sts
St st 17 rows straight

To shape forehead

Dec 1 st at each end of row and every
alt row until 12 sts, mark each end of
this row with coloured thread then
Dec 1 st at each end of following alt
row (10 sts).

To shape nose

St st 13 rows
Dec 1 st at each end of next 2 rows

Cast off, knitting 2 sts tog at each end
of row at same time.

Ears

make 4

Cast on 15 sts and St st 4 rows
Dec 1 st at each end of next row and
each following alt row until 9 sts
Dec 1 st at each end of next row
Cast off remaining 7 sts, knitting 2 sts
tog at each end of row at same time.

Arm
Side A
make 2

Cast on 5 sts Start with a K row
Inc 1 st at each end of every row until
17 sts
ROW 7—K
ROW 8—P
ROW 9—Inc 1 st at beg of row and Dec
1 st at end of row
ROW 10—P
Rep last 2 rows 5 times
ROW 21—Dec 1 st at end of row and
following alt row (15 sts)
ROW 24—P **
ROW 25—Inc 1 st at beg and Dec 1 st
at end of row
St st 9 rows (ending at back edge)
ROW 35—Inc 1 st at beg of row and
following 10 th row (17 sts)
St st 9 rows (ending on a P row)
ROW 55—Inc 1 st at each end of row
(19 sts)
St st 13 rows
Dec 1 st at each end of row and every
row until 9 sts
Cast off, purling 2 sts tog at each end
of row at same time.

Arm
Side B
make 2

Cast on 5 sts Start with a K row
Inc 1 st at each end of every row until
17 sts
ROW 7—K
ROW 8—P
ROW 9—Dec 1 st at beg of row and Inc
1 st at end of row
ROW 10—P
Rep last 2 rows 5 times
ROW 21—Dec 1 st at beg of row and
following alt row (15 sts)
ROW 24—P **
ROW 25—Dec 1 st at beg and Inc 1 st
at end of row
St st 9 rows
ROW 35—Inc 1 st at end of row and
following 10 th row (17 sts)
St st 9 rows (ending on a P row)
ROW 55—Inc 1 st at each end of row
St st 13 rows
ROW 69—Dec 1 st at each end of row
and every row until 9 sts
Cast off as first arm

Contrast paw pads

Catherine does not have contrast paw
pads, but if you like them, make one
of the pairs of arms using a contrast
colour up to ** and then change to
main colour.

Legs
Side A
make 2
To shape heel and toe

Cast on 34 sts
Starting with a P row, St st 3 rows
ROW 4—Dec 1 st at beg of row and 2
following alt rows (31 sts)

ROW 9—P
ROW 10—Dec 1 st at each end of row
ROW 11—Dec 1 st at end of row (28 sts)
ROW 12—Cast off 8 sts at beg of row (slipping the first st) and Dec 1 st at end of row (19 sts)
ROW 13—Dec 1 st at end of row
ROW 14—Dec 1 st at beg of row
ROW 15—P
ROW 16—Dec 1 st at each end of row (15 sts)
St st 5 rows (ending on a P row)
ROW 22—Inc 1 st at beg of row and following 4 th row (17 sts)
St st 5 rows
ROW 32—Inc 1 st at each end of row and following 4 th row (21 sts)
St st 5 rows (ending on a P row)
ROW 42—Inc 1 st at beg of row and following 4 th row (23 sts)
St st 9 rows
ROW 56—Dec 1 st at each end of row and every alt row until 17 sts, then every row until 11 sts
Cast off, knitting 2 sts tog at each end of row at same time

Legs
Side B
make 2
To shape heel and toe
Cast on 34 sts
Starting with a K row, st st 3 rows
ROW 4—Dec 1 st at beg of row and 2 following alt rows (31 sts)
ROW 9—K
ROW 10—Dec 1 st at each end of row (29 sts)
ROW 11—Dec 1 st at end of row
ROW 12—Cast off 8 sts at beg of row (slipping the first st) and Dec 1 st at

end of row (19 sts)
ROW 13—Dec 1 st at end of row
ROW 14—Dec 1 st at beg of row (17 sts)
ROW 15—K
ROW 16—Dec 1 st at each end of row (15 sts)
St st 5 rows (ending on a K row)
ROW 22—Inc 1 st at beg of row and following 4 th row
St st 5 rows
ROW 32—Inc 1 st at each end of row and following 4 th row (21 sts)
St st 5 rows (ending on a K row)
ROW 42—Inc 1 st at beg of row and following 4 th row (23 sts)
St st 9 rows, ending on a K row
Dec 1 st at each end of row and every alt row until 17 sts, and then on every row until 11 sts
Cast off purling 2 sts tog at each end of row at the same time

Soles
make 2
Cast on 5 sts
ROW 1—Inc 1 st at each end of row and every following alt row until 15 sts
St st 21 rows
ROW 36—Dec 1 st at each end of row and every following alt row until 5 sts
Cast off slipping the first st

To knit nose
With fingering (4-ply) yarn and size 2 (2¾mm) needles, cast on 6 sts
ROW 1—Inc 1, K to last 2 sts, Inc 1, K1
ROW 2—Purl
Rep the last 2 rows until 12 sts
Cast off, leaving a long thread to sew

nose to head

To make up
Do not press.
Sew all the pieces together with K sides facing and use a small backstitch about 1 st from the edge (unless otherwise stated).

Body
Pin the two body pieces together, matching the back markers. Sew all round, leaving a gap between markers for turning and stuffing.

Head
Pin and sew the two head pieces from front neck to nose. Pin, adjust and sew in the head gusset matching the eye markers and making sure the tip of the nose is accurately in line with the chin seam.

Before putting in the safety eyes, stuff the head but don't be too fussy yet as it is only temporary while you check that you are happy with the eye positions. Push the eyes between the stitches into the face at the markers, then decide if you like them there. Try moving them about a stitch at a time, until you like the look of your bear. Remove the stuffing and attach the safety washers.

Now stuff the head carefully and firmly, starting with the nose, moulding and shaping until you are happy with the size and shape.

Sew the ear pieces right sides together around the curved edges, leaving the bottom edges open. Turn right side out and oversew closed.

Pin the ears towards the back of

the head, halfway across each head gusset seam and curving inwards. Sew on with body coloured yarn. Pin and sew on the nose with the attached thread and using the photograph of Catherine as a guide.

With black embroidery thread, sew a mouth with 3 small sts.

Limbs

Match up, pin and sew the arm and leg pieces together, leaving approx. 2 inches (5cm) open at the back for turning and stuffing and inserting joints. Sew in the soles and turn all pieces right side out.

Carefully stuff the limbs about half way up for now. Sew on claws using nose coloured yarn (see General Instructions on page 13).

Inserting and attaching safety joints

Most of the bears in this book are quite small and only require thread or button "joints". Catherine and Jack, however, are traditionally made bears and will look better with plastic safety joints for their head and limbs.

Attaching joints

The plastic joints come in two halves. The shanked half is placed snugly inside the top of the limbs with the shank pushed through the stitching to the outside (be careful not to break any stitches while doing this). To find the exact spot where to push the shank through, first place the joint against the outside of the limb, right at the top, so that there is very little room around the sides, then put a pin

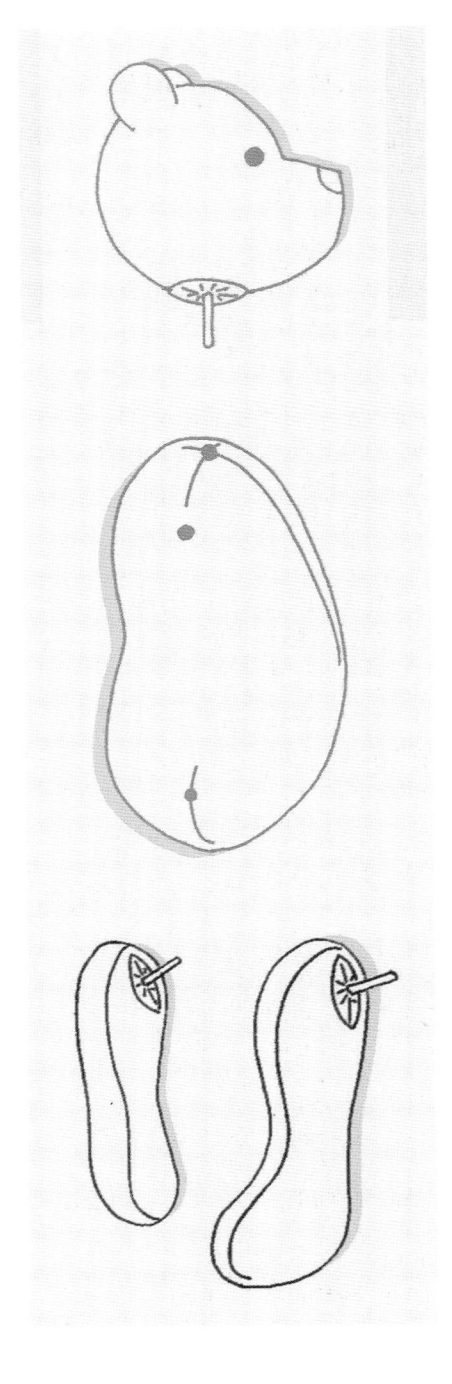

or marker where the shank of the joint is to go through. Fix the joints into place, finish stuffing the limbs and close the gap with a ladderstitch. The head joint is fixed in a similar way after stuffing the head and then the gathered neck edge is pulled up tightly around the shank and oversewn a number of times to secure.

Attaching head and limbs

All the joints are fixed into place on the body before it is stuffed, but it is a good idea to quickly stuff temporarily for now while you try out your joint positions. As a guide, the arm joint shanks are fixed about ½ inch (1cm) below beginning of shoulder shaping (which you should be able to see). The leg joints about ½ inch (1cm) below end of hip shaping. The head joint shaft goes through the centre top of the body where all the seam ends meet. You could try using a thin knitting needle pushed through the limbs and body to see how they will look. Push the shanks carefully through the stitching of the body, then if you change your mind and pull them out, the holes will close up and you can try again. When you are happy with the look of them and teddy can sit comfortably, remove the body stuffing and push the washers firmly home onto the shanks. Now stuff firmly and close the final seam.

Dress
Front

With size 2 (2¾mm) knitting needles and white 4-ply cotton, cast on 116 sts and work 2 rows in G. st (both rows K)

Work 4 rows of pattern panel A as follows:

Pattern panel A

ROW 1—K2, yfwd, S11, K2 tog, psso, K1, *(yfwd, K1) twice, S11, K2 tog, psso, K1, rep from * to last 2 sts, yfwd, K2

ROW 2—P

ROWS 3 AND 4—Rep the last 2 rows

St st 7 rows (ending on a K row)

Work 3 rows of eyelet pattern as follows:

Eyelet pattern—B

ROW 1—K

ROW 2—K1, (yfwd, K2 tog) to last st, K1

ROW 3—K

Starting with a K row, St st 4 rows

Rep the 4 rows of pattern panel A

St st 3 rows (ending on K row)

Rep the 3 eyelet rows (pattern B)

Continue in St st until skirt measures 8½ inches (21cm), (ending on a P row)

Dec row and shaping bodice

NEXT ROW—K2, K2 tog to last 2 sts, K2 (60 sts)

Cast off 7 sts at beg of next 2 rows (46 sts)

Work the eyelet and pattern rows as follows:

Eyelet rows

ROW 1—K

ROW 2—K2, *K2 tog, yfwd, rep from * to last 2 sts, K2

ROW 3—K**

St st 4 rows

Pattern panel

ROW 1—K3, yfwd, S11, K2 tog, psso, K1, *(yfwd, K1) twice, S11, K2 tog, psso, K1, rep from * to last 3 sts, yfwd, K3

ROW 2—P

ROWS 3 AND 4—Rep last 2 rows once

St st 3 rows (ending on a K row)

Rep the 3 eyelet rows

St st straight until work measures 2¾ inches (7cm) from start of armholes, ending on a P row.

To shape neck

NEXT ROW—K18 sts, turn and work on these sts only for now

Dec 1 st at neck edge on next 3 rows, then on the following 4 alt rows (11 sts)

St st a further 7 rows straight

Cast off

With right side facing, place the next 10 sts on a holder for now, rejoin yarn to remaining sts and K to end

Complete to match first side.

Back

Work as for front to ** (end of first set of eyelet rows on bodice).

St st straight until bodice back matches front to shoulders ending on a P row.

To shape shoulders

Cast off 6 sts at beg of next 2 rows, then 5 sts at beg of following 2 rows.

Work 3 rows in G. st.

Cast off.

To make up

Press pieces well using a damp cloth.

Neckline

With size 2 (2¾mm) needles and right side facing, pick up and knit 14 sts evenly along left side of neck, K across 10 sts on holder, then pick up and K 14 sts along right side of neck.

Work 3 rows G. st

Cast off.

Right side of dress

Join right shoulder seam, then, with right side facing and starting at armhole edge, pick up and knit 80 sts evenly around entire armhole, (front and back).

G. st 3 rows and cast off.

Sew up right skirt seam.

Left side of dress

With right side facing, pick up and knit 16 sts along left back shoulder (including neck edging)

G. st 3 rows and cast off

Work the front shoulder in the same way with the addition of a buttonhole row in the 2 nd row

BUTTONHOLE ROW—K4, yfwd, K2 tog, K5, yfwd, K2 tog, K3

Sew up left skirt seam.

Finally, starting at the top of the shoulder, pick up and K 80 sts evenly around entire armhole and complete to match right side.

Sew on 2 buttons.

Jack

Black bears were made and given as mourning bears for survivors of the *Titanic* disaster in 1912. The unusual colour was not very popular at the time but is now very collectable and the original bears are extremely expensive. I wanted a similar one for myself, so here he is. Not mohair, of course, but still handsome enough.

Materials

• Approx **2 x 2oz balls fingering (2 x 50g 4-ply) yarn** in dark grey
• Approx **1oz fingering (30g 4-ply) yarn** in cream for the pads of the feet
• A pair of **US 2 (2¾mm) knitting needles**
• Approx **9oz (250g) polyester stuffing**
• Size **¼ inch (5mm) safety eyes**
• **5 x 2 inch (45mm) plastic safety joints**
• **A tapestry or wool needle** for sewing up bear
• **Black embroidery thread** for nose, mouth and claws
• **Ribbon** to tie around neck

Height

Approx 15 inches (38cm).

Follow the instructions for Catherine (see pages 49–53) with the exception of the knitted nose. Use the contrast colour for the soles and up to ** on 1 pair of arms. Using black embroidery thread, darn a nose, mouth and claws.

Ralph

This busy little bear is wondering if it is teatime. He would make an unusual gift for an adult or an amusing addition to your bear collection.

Materials
- Approx **2oz fingering (50g 4-ply) yarn** in the colour of your choice for the bear
- Approx **2oz fingering (50g 4-ply) yarn** in the colour of your choice for the jeans
- Approx **1oz fingering (30g 4-ply) yarn in brown** for the belt
- **1 press fastener** (optional) for the belt
- Approx **1oz fingering (30g 4-ply) yarn** in the colour of your choice for vest
- **A pair of size US 2 (2¾mm) knitting needles** for bear and clothes
- **2 small black beads** for eyes or ¼ inch (5mm) teddy looped-back eyes
- **Strong black thread** for attaching bead or teddy eyes
- Approx **1oz (30g) of polyester stuffing**
- **A tapestry or wool needle** for sewing up and embroidering nose, mouth and claws
- **Black or dark brown embroidery thread** for nose, mouth and claws
- **2 holders** for vest

The bear shown was made using Jaeger Matchmaker Merino 4-ply in Soft Camel (718) and Jaeger Matchmaker Merino 4-ply in Baltic Blue (740).

Height
Approx 10 inches (25cm).

Work in St st throughout unless otherwise stated.

Body and Head
Side A
make 1
With main colour, cast on 9 sts
To shape bottom and tummy
Starting with a K row, Inc 1 st at each end of every row until 19 sts
ROW 6—P
ROW 7—(Inc 1, K2), to last st, Inc 1 (26 sts)
ROW 8—P
ROW 9—Inc 1 st at end of row
St st 11 rows (ending on a P row)
ROW 21—Dec 1 st at beg of row and each following alt row until 23 sts
ROW 28—P
ROW 29—Dec 1 st at end of row and each following alt row until 19 sts
ROW 36—P
ROW 37—Inc 1 st at beg and Dec 1 st at end of row
ROW 38—P
To shape chest and shoulders
ROW 39—Dec 1 st at end of row and each alt row until 15 sts
ROW 46—P
ROW 47—Dec 1 st at each end of row and following alt row (11 sts)
ROW 50—Dec 1 st at end of row
St st 2 rows, ending on a P row

To shape head
ROW 53—Inc 1 st at end of row
ROW 54—Cast on 6 sts, P to end
ROW 55—Inc 1 st at end of row (18 sts)
ROW 56—Inc 1 st at beg of row
ROW 57—Inc 1 st at end of row (20 sts)
St st 7 rows (ending on a P row)
ROW 65—Dec 1 st at beg of row
To shape nose
ROW 66—Cast off 5 sts, P to last 2 sts, P2 tog (13 sts)
ROW 67—Dec 1 st at each end of row and following row (9 sts)
Cast off, knitting 2 sts tog at each end of row at same time.

Body and Head
Side B
make 1
With main colour, cast on 9 sts
Starting with a P row, Inc 1 st at each end of every row until 19 sts
ROW 6—K
ROW 7—(Inc 1, P2) to last st, Inc 1 (26 sts)
ROW 8—K
ROW 9—Inc 1 st at end of row
St st 11 rows (ending on a K row)
ROW 21—Dec 1 st at beg of row and each following alt row until 23 sts
ROW 28—K
ROW 29—Dec 1 st at end of row and each following alt row until 19 sts
ROW 36—K
ROW 37—Inc 1 st at beg and Dec 1 st at end of row
ROW 38—K

To shape chest and shoulders

ROW 39—Dec 1 st at end of row and each alt row until 15 sts

ROW 46—K

ROW 47—Dec 1 st at each end of row and following alt row (11 sts)

ROW 50—Dec 1 st at end of row

St st 2 rows, ending with a K row

To shape head

ROW 53—Inc 1 st at end of row

ROW 54—Cast on 6 sts, K to end (17 sts)

ROW 55—Inc 1 st at end of row

ROW 56—Inc 1 st at beg of row

ROW 57—Inc 1 st at end of row (20 sts)

St st 7 rows (ending on a K row)

ROW 65—Dec 1 st at beg of row

To shape nose

ROW 66—Cast off 5 sts, K to last 2 sts, K2 tog (13 sts)

ROW 67—Dec 1 st at each end of row and following row (9 sts)

Cast off in P, working 2 sts tog at each end of row at the same time.

Head Gusset

make 1

With main colour, cast on 3 sts P 1 row

Inc 1 st at each end of row and every alt row until 13 sts

St st 9 rows (ending on a P row)

To shape nose

Dec 1 st at each end of next 3 rows (7 sts)

St st 11 rows

Next row K2 tog at each end of row

Cast off in P

Ears

make 2

With main colour cast on 9 sts,

working in G. st:

K 5 rows

Dec 1 st at each end of row and following alt row

Cast off, knitting 2 sts tog at each end of row at same time, leaving a long thread

Arms

make 2

With main colour cast on 6 sts

ROW 1—Inc 1, K1, Inc in next 2 sts, K1, Inc 1 (10 sts)

ROW 2—Inc 1, P3, Inc in next 2 sts, P3, Inc 1 (14 sts)

ROW 3—Inc 1, K5, Inc in next 2 sts, K5, Inc 1 (18 sts)

ROW 4—P

ROW 5—Inc 1 st at each end of next and following alt row (22 sts)

ROW 8—P

ROW 9—Inc 1, K8, K2 tog twice, K8, Inc 1

ROW 10—P

ROW 11—K9, K2 tog twice, K9

ROW 12—P

ROW 13—K8, K2 tog twice, K8

ROW 14—P7, P2 tog twice, P7

Inc 1 st at each end of next and every following 12 th row until 22 sts

St st 11 rows straight

ROW 51—K2 tog, K7, K2 tog twice, K7, K2 tog

ROW 52—P2 tog, P5, P2 tog twice, P5, P2 tog (14 sts)

Cast off, knitting 2 sts together at each end of row at same time

Legs

make 2

With main colour cast on 36 sts,

Starting with a K row, St st 4 rows

To shape toes

ROW 5—Dec 1 st at each end of row and following alt row (32 sts)

ROW 8—P

Cast off 8 sts at beg of next 2 rows, slipping the first st each time

ROW 11—Inc 1 st at each end of row and every 4 th row until 26 sts

St st 6 rows

ROW 34—P2 tog, P9, P2 tog twice, P9, P2 tog

ROW 35—K

ROW 36—P2 tog, P7, P2 tog twice, P7, P2 tog

Cast off remaining 18 sts, knitting 2 sts tog at each end of row at same time.

Soles

make 2

With main colour cast on 4 sts

Starting with a K row, inc 1 st at each end of next 3 rows (10 sts)

St st 15 rows

Dec 1 st at each end of next 3 rows

Cast off remaining 4 sts in P, slipping the first st.

To make up

Press all the pieces on the purl side to make sewing up easier.

Head and Body

With K sides together make up following the instructions for *Annie & George* on page 20.

Ears

Sew in and trim off the shorter cast on thread. Thread the longer thread onto the needle; weave it in along the edge of the ear down to the corner and pull slightly to give a rounded shape. Anchor the thread using a couple of sts and use the rest to sew the ears to the head. Pin in position first, about ¾ inch (1cm) in from the back of the head and about halfway across the head gusset seam.

Eyes

See General Instructions on page 13.

Nose and Mouth

Use three strands of black or dark brown embroidery thread to sew a nose and your choice of mouth.

Legs

With K sides together, fold each leg in half lengthways, pin, then sew around the top and down the front, leaving a small gap (about ¾ inch or 2cm) for stuffing and the bottom edges open. Pin, adjust, and sew the soles to the feet. Turn out and stuff. Check each pair of limbs is the same size, then sew up the gap in the seams, using ladder st.

Arms

With K sides together, fold each arm lengthways and sew up the back seam, leaving a small gap for turning and stuffing. Turn out and stuff lightly. Close gap.

Claws

Make three or four little claws on each paw with black or dark brown embroidery thread.

Thread-joining

See General Instructions on page 13.

Vest

Front

With vest colour cast on 30 sts
St st 12 rows

To shape armholes

Starting with a K row, St st 12 rows
Cast off 4 sts at beg of next 2 rows
Dec 1 st at each end of next and following alt row (18 sts) *
St st 3 rows

To shape first side of neck

NEXT ROW—K 6, turn and work on these sts only for now
Dec 1 st at neck edge on next 2 rows (4 sts)
**St st 5 rows
Cast off

To shape second side of neck

With right side facing, place the next 6 sts on a holder for front neck, then rejoin yarn and K to end to match first side shaping.

Back

Work as for front to *
St st 5 rows

To shape neck

Follow shaping and complete as for front neck except St st 3 rows at ** instead of 5

To make up

Darn in and trim loose threads and press both the pieces. Join the right shoulder seam. With right sides facing, and vest colour pick up and knit 9 sts down left front neck, K across the 6 sts on first holder, pick up and K 9 sts up right front neck, 7 sts down right back neck, 6 sts from holder and 7 sts up left back neck.(44 sts) Work 1 row of single rib and cast off. Join left shoulder and side seams.

Jeans

make 2 pieces

Starting at bottom of leg
With jeans colour, cast on 36 sts and
G. st 2 rows

To shape crotch

Starting with a K row, St st 16 rows
Cast off 2 sts at beg of next 2 rows
St st a further 22 rows
NEXT ROW—K3, (K2 tog, K2) to last 5 sts, K2 tog, K3 (25 sts)
G. st 3 rows
Cast off

Pockets

With jeans colour cast on 10 sts
K 1 row
Starting with a K row, St st 8 rows
Cast off

Belt

With brown cast on 3 sts and G. st until belt measures about 8 inches (20cm) Cast off
Sew half the press fastener to one end of the belt and the other half about ¾ inch (2cm) in from the other end (on the opposite side) so that when fastened some of the belt hangs loose.

To make up

With right sides together, fold each leg in half lengthways and sew up leg seam (shortest length of work is legs) Turn one leg right way out and fit this one inside the other. Sew up crotch seam and turn right side out. Sew on pockets.

Sleepy Sam

This pattern is based on a combination of Ralph and Christopher with slight alterations to the head and legs. He is knitted in a worsted-weight (D/K) yarn to make him a bit larger. I have also added a few pellets to give him a beanie bag effect which makes him more poseable. A bag of plastic pellets can be purchased from most haberdashery or craft stores.

Materials
- Approx **2oz worsted (50g D/K-weight) yarn** in the colour of your choice for the bear
- Approx **1oz worsted (30g D/K-weight) yarn** in the colour of your choice for paw pads and soles
- 1 pair **US size 3 (3mm) knitting needles**
- Approx **1½ oz (40g) polyester stuffing**
- Approx **1 cupful (1 tablespoon) plastic pellets** (optional)
- **Dark brown embroidery thread** for eyes, nose, mouth and claws

Height
Approximately 10 inches (25cm).

Head and Body
Side A
Follow instructions for Ralph up to row 52.

To shape head
ROW 53—K
ROW 54—Inc 1 st at each end of row
ROW 55—K
ROW 56—Inc 1 st at beg of row
ROW 57—K
ROW 58—Cast on 4 sts at beg of row (17 sts), P to end
ROW 59—Inc 1 st at end of row
ROW 60—Inc 1 st at beg of row
ROW 61—Inc 1 st at end of row (20 sts)
St st 5 rows (finishing on a P row)
ROW 67—Dec 1 st at beg of row
ROW 68—Cast off 8 sts at beg of row and Dec 1 st at end of row (10 sts)
ROW 69—Dec 1 st at beg of row
Dec 1 st at each end of next 2 rows
ROW 72—Cast off remaining sts, purling 2 sts tog at each end of row at the same time

Head and Body
Side B
Follow the instructions for Ralph to row 52

To shape head
ROW 53—P

ROW 54—Inc 1 st at each end of row
ROW 55—P
ROW 56—Inc 1 st at beg of row
ROW 57—P
ROW 58—Cast on 4 sts at beg of row (17 sts), K to end
ROW 59—Inc 1 st at end of row
ROW 60—Inc 1 st at beg of row
ROW 61—Inc 1 st at end of row (20 sts)
St st 5 rows (finishing on a K row)
ROW 67—Dec 1 st at beg of row
ROW 68—Cast off 8 sts at beg of row and Dec 1 st at end of row (10 sts)
ROW 69—Dec 1 st at beg of row
Dec 1 st at each end of next 2 rows
ROW 72—Cast off remaining 5 sts, knitting 2 sts tog at each end of row at the same time

Head Gussett
Cast on 3 sts and beg with a K row, st st 2 rows
Inc 1 st at each end of the next and each following 6 th row until 11 sts
St st 11 rows
Dec 1 st each end of next 2 rows
St st 6 rows
Dec 1 st at each end of next row (5 sts)
Cast off, slipping the first st

Ears
Cast on 8 sts and g. st 3 rows
Dec 1 st at each end of next 2 rows
Cast off, slipping the first st

Legs
make 2

With main colour cast on 34 sts,
Starting with a K row, st st 4 rows

To shape toes

ROW 5—Dec 1 st at each end of row and following alt row (30 sts)
ROW 8—P
Cast off 6 sts at beg of next 2 rows
ROW 11—Inc 1 st at each end of row and every 4 th row until 26 sts
St st 6 rows

ROW 30—P2 tog, P9, P2 tog twice, P9, P2 tog
ROW 31—K
ROW 32—P2 tog, P7, P2 tog twice, P7, P2 tog
Cast off remaining 18 sts, knitting 2 sts tog at each end of row at the same time

Soles

As for Christopher bear (see page 25).

Arms

As for Christopher bear arms (see page 24).

To make up

Sew up all the pieces following the instructions for Christopher (page 25), replacing some of the stuffing with pellets in the body. Thread-joint fairly loosely. I have sewn his ears a little bit lower down on his head and used 2 strands of embroidery thread to make a small stitch for each eye.

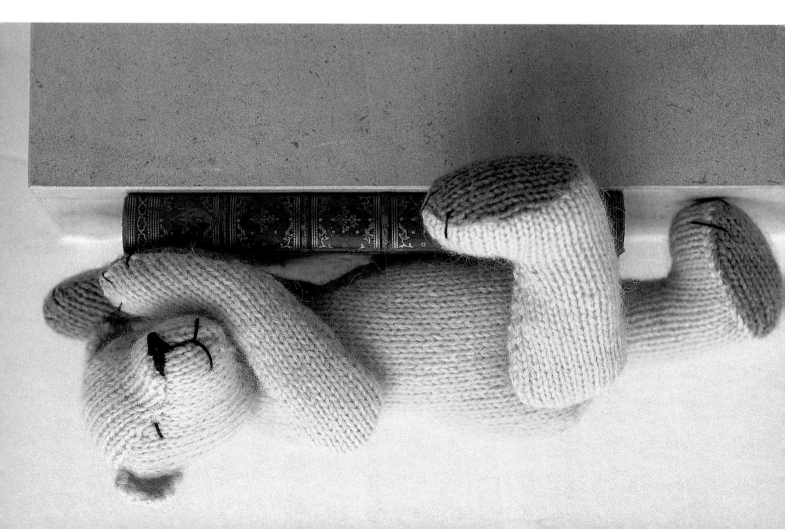

Bertie & Bruce

These little bears have long bodies and short arms and legs, similar to teddy bears made in the 1940s and 50s. Their arms and legs are each made in one piece, so they are very quick to make.
They are knitted in a D/K yarn on US 3 (3mm) needles, and their clothes are knitted in fingering yarn (4-ply).

The bears shown are knitted in Rowan Kid Classic D/K in Bear (817) for Bertie and Jaeger Baby Merino D/K Gold (225) for Bruce. The jumper is knitted in Jaeger Matchmaker Merino 4-ply in Cream (662) and Blood (705) and the shorts in Baltic Blue (740).

Materials
- Approx 2oz worsted (50g D/K) yarn in the colour of your choice for Bertie
- Approx 2oz worsted (50g D/K) yarn in the colour of your choice for Bruce
- 1 pair US 3 (3mm) knitting needles for the bears
- 1 pair ¼ inch (5mm) teddy looped-back eyes or beads and strong black thread
- Approx 1oz (30g) polyester stuffing
- Brown or black embroidery thread for nose, mouth and claws (and eyes if bear is for a child)
- Approx 1oz fingering (30g 4-ply) yarn in the colours of your choice for the clothes
- 1 pair each of US 1 (2¼mm) and US 2 (2¾mm) knitting needles for the clothes
- 2 small buttons for shorts
- 1 safety pin for jumper

Head and Body

Height
Approximately 9 inches (23cm).

Work in St st throughout and start each piece with a K row unless otherwise stated.

Side A
make 1
With main colour cast on 4 sts
Starting with a K row
Row 1—Inc in each st
Row 2—P
Row 3—Inc 1, K2, Inc in next 2 sts, K2, Inc 1
Row 4—P
Row 5—Inc 1, K4, Inc in next 2 sts, K4, Inc 1
Row 6—P
Row 7—Inc 1, K6, Inc in next 2 sts, K6, Inc 1
Row 8—P
Row 9—K9, Inc in next 2 sts, K9
Row 10—P
Row 11—K10, Inc in next 2 sts, K10
St st 19 rows **

To shape shoulders
Row 31—Sl 1, K2 tog, K to end
Row 32—P
Row 33—K9, K2 tog twice, K10
St st 3 rows
Row 37—K8, K2 tog twice, K9
Row 38—P
Row 39—Sl 1, K2 tog, K4, K2 tog twice, K5, K2 tog, K1
Row 40—P6, P2 tog twice, P5
Row 41—Sl 1, K2 tog, K1, K2 tog twice, K2, K2 tog, K1
Row 42—P

To shape head
Row 43—K
Row 44—Inc 1 st at each end of row and following alt row (13 sts)
Row 47—Inc 1 st at beg of row
Row 48—Inc 1 st at end of row
Rep last 2 rows twice (19 sts)
St st 4 rows (ending on a P row)

To shape nose
Row 57—Cast off 3 sts at beg of row
Row 58—Dec 1 st at end of row
Row 59—Cast off 3 sts at beg of row (12 sts) mark last cast off st with a coloured thread
Row 60—Dec 1 st at beg of row
Row 61—K
Row 62—Dec 1 st at each end of this and following row
Cast off remaining 7 sts, purling 2 sts together at each end of row at same time.

Head and Body

Side B
Work as for side A until **

To shape shoulders
Row 31—K to last 3 sts, K2 tog, K1
Row 32—P

ROW 33—K10, K2 tog twice, K9
St st 3 rows
ROW 37—K9, tog twice, K8
ROW 38—P
ROW 39—Sl 1, K2 tog, K5, K2 tog twice, K4, K2 tog, K1
ROW 40—P5, P2 tog twice, P6
ROW 41—Sl 1, K2 tog, K2, K2tog twice, K1, K2 tog, K1 (9 sts)
ROW 42—P

To shape head

ROW 43—Inc 1 st at each end of row and following alt row
ROW 46—Inc 1 st at beg of row
ROW 47—Inc 1 st at end of row
Rep last 2 rows twice (19 sts)
St st 4 rows (ending on a K row)

To shape nose

ROW 56—Cast off 3 sts at beg of row
ROW 57—Dec 1 st at end of row
ROW 58—Cast off 3 sts at beg of row, slipping the first st. mark last cast off st with a coloured thread
ROW 59—Dec 1 st at beg of row
ROW 60—P
ROW 61—Dec 1 st at each end of this and following row
Cast off remaining 7 sts, knitting 2 sts tog at each end of row at same time

Head Gusset

Starting at back neck edge
Cast on 2 sts and starting with a K row,
Inc in each st (4 sts)
P 1 row
Inc 1 st at each end of next and every 4 th row until 12 sts
St st 9 rows (ending on a P row)

To shape nose

Dec 1 st at each end of next and every alt row until 6 sts, mark each end of last row with a coloured thread
St st 5 more rows
NEXT ROW—K2 tog, K2, K2 tog
Cast off, slipping the first st

Ears

Each 1 piece—make 2
Cast on 9 sts
Starting with a K row St st 3 rows
Dec 1 st at each end of next 2 rows
Inc 1 st at each end of next 2 rows
St st 3 rows
Cast off

Arms

make 2
To shape paws
Cast on 8 sts
ROW 1—Inc 1, K2, Inc in next 2 sts, K2, Inc 1
ROW 2—P
ROW 3—Inc 1, K4, Inc in next 2 sts, K4, Inc 1
ROW 4—P
ROW 5—Inc 1 st at each end of row (18 sts)
ROW 6—P
ROW 7—Inc 1, K6, K 2 tog twice, K6, Inc 1
ROW 8—P
Repeat the last 2 rows once
ROW 11—K7, K2 tog twice, K7 (16 sts)
St st 7 rows
ROW 19—K7, Inc in next 2 sts, K7
St st 11 rows
ROW 31—K2 tog, K5, K2 tog twice, K5, K2 tog
ROW 32—P2 tog, P3, P2 tog twice, P3, P2 tog
Cast off, slipping the first st

Legs

make 2
Cast on 28 sts and starting with a K row, St st 4 rows
Dec 1 st at each end of next 5 rows (18 sts)
St st 3 rows
ROW 13—Inc 1 st at each end of row and following 6 th row (22 sts)
St st 7 rows
ROW 27—K2 tog, K7, K2 tog twice, K7, K2 tog
ROW 28—P
ROW 29—K2 tog, K5, K2 tog twice,

Arms

With right sides together, pin and sew up each arm, leaving a small gap for turning and stuffing. Turn right side out and stuff carefully. Check that both the arms have the same amount of stuffing in, then close the gap.

Legs

Sew up the legs in the same way as the arms but leave the bottom edges open. Pin, adjust and sew in the soles. Turn right side out and stuff.

Inserting the Head Gusset

Working in good light, pin, adjust and sew one side of the gusset to one side of the head, matching the marker. Make sure that the centre of the nose end of the gusset matches the centre seam of nose on the head. Repeat with the other side. The two markers are the approximate position for the eyes. Sew from "c" to "d". Turn out, stuff carefully and close back seam. Tie a piece of the same coloured yarn around the neck and pull fairly tightly to further define the head and shoulders.

Inserting the Eyes

Follow the instructions given in General Instructions on page 13 for inserting loop-back eyes. For a young child, use black or brown embroidery thread and oversew some tiny sts on top of each other.

Nose, Mouth and Claws

Using black or brown embroidery thread, satin stitch a triangle shape for the nose and shape the mouth with two or three stitches. There are some examples of features in the general instructions.

Sew three or four stitches on the edge of each paw for the claws.

Ears

Fold each ear with right sides together, sew up one side, run thread through top of ear, pulling very slightly to curve ear, then sew down other side and fasten off.

Turn right side out and oversew bottom edges closed.

To make up

Press lightly if necessary. With right sides together, pin and sew the 2 body and head pieces together from the nose, down around the chin and tummy and up to the middle of the back (see diagram above).

Soles
make 2

Cast on 3 sts

Starting with a K row, inc 1 st at each end of row and following alt row (7 sts)

St st 10 rows

Dec 1 st at each end of row and following alt row (3 sts)

NEXT ROW—K2 tog, K1, pass 1 st over the other and finish off

K5, K2 tog (14 sts)

Cast off, purling 2 sts tog at each end of row at same time.

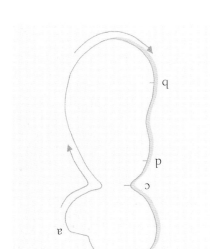

check that both legs are the same size and sew up the gap.

Attaching the Limbs

You can attach the arms and legs using one of the methods described in the general instructions. I find that thread-jointing looks the best and it is quite easy once you have had a bit of practise. If the bear is intended for a child though, he will probably be cuddled quite a bit so you may have to stitch the insides of the limbs firmly to the body with some extra strong thread or plenty of yarn.

Striped Sweater
Pattern

All rib is worked in cream and stripes are of 2 rows each, beginning with red.

Back
make 1

With size 1 (2¼mm) needles and cream, cast on 32 sts and work 4 rows in single rib
Change to size 2 (2¾mm) needles and St st 14 rows in 2 row stripes, starting with red. Place a marker at each end of last row
Keeping the striped pattern correct throughout, Dec 1 st at each end of next 4 rows (24 sts) **
St st straight for 16 rows

To shape shoulders

Cast off 5 sts at beg of next 2 rows (14 sts)
Change back to size 1 (2¼mm) needles and work 4 rows in rib then cast off loosely in rib

Front
make 1

Work as back to **
St st straight for 9 rows

To shape right side of neck

NEXT ROW—P8, turn and work on these sts for now (you will need to break cream yarn)
Dec 1 st at neck edge on next 3 rows (5 sts)
St st 4 rows, ending at side edge
Cast off

To shape left side of neck

With wrong side facing, place next 8 sts on a safety pin, rejoin cream and P to end.
Complete to match left side of work.

Sleeves
make 2

With size 1 (2¼mm) needles and cream, cast on 31 sts and rib 2 rows
Change to size 2 (2¾mm) needles and St st 3 rows
Inc 1 st at each end of next row
St st 2 more rows and place markers at each end of last row

To shape armholes

Dec 1 st at each end of next 4 rows (25 sts)
Cast off (in red)

To make up

Press the pieces lightly then darn in and neaten off the loose threads
With right side of work facing and using size 1 (2¼mm) needles and cream, pick up and K 8 sts evenly along left side of neck

K across 8 sts on safety pin, then pick up and knit 8 sts along right side of neck. Rib 4 rows on these 24 sts then cast off loosely in rib
Join front and back shoulder seams (including neck rib) and the side seams up to markers.
Join sleeve seams to markers.
Sew in sleeves K sides together, matching seams and turn right side out.

Shorts
Right Side

Starting at waistband
With size 1 (2¼mm) needles and blue, cast on 30 sts and work in single rib for 2 rows
BUTTONHOLE ROW—Rib 5, yfwd, K2 tog, rib to end
Rib 2 more rows *
Change to size size 2 (2¾mm) needles

To shape back

NEXT ROW—K5, turn and purl back
NEXT ROW—K10, purl back
NEXT ROW—K15, purl back
K across all sts and then St st a further 17 rows straight, ending on a P row. Mark each end of this row

To shape legs

NEXT ROW—Inc 1 st at each end of next and following alt row (34 sts)
P 1 row
G. st 3 rows
Cast off

Left Side

Work as for right side to *
Change to size 2 (2¾mm) needles

To shape back

NEXT ROW—P5, turn and knit back

NEXT ROW—P10, knit back

NEXT ROW—P15, knit back

P across all sts

Complete to match right side

Straps

Make 2 straps with size 2 (2¾mm) needles and blue, cast on 4 sts and work in single rib until straps measure 6 inches (15cm) or until they will fit from front to back waistband, crossed at back and with about ½ inch (1cm) extra for buttoning up.

To make up

Darn in and trim loose threads. Press pieces lightly. Fold each side in half and join the inside leg seams up to the markers. Turn one piece the right way out, place inside the other piece and sew up the crotch seam from the front waistband to the back. Sew one end of straps just inside the back waistband about ½ inch (1cm) either side of the centre back seam. Sew a button on the other end of straps.

Elizabeth & Heidi

These are delicate little teddies that look very pretty in their tiny clothes. They are made up in reverse stocking stitch, which means that you sew up the finished pieces with purl sides together. To ensure a good fit, the clothes for Elizabeth and Heidi should be made using the same brand of yarn as used for the bears.

Materials
- Approx **1oz fingering (30g 4-ply) yarn** in the colour of your choice for each bear
- Approx **1oz fingering (30g 4-ply) yarn** in a contrast colour for paw pads and soles
- Approx **1oz fingering (30g 4-ply) yarn** in the colour of your choice for the cardigan and dress
- A pair of **US 1 (2¼mm) knitting needles** for bears
- A pair of **US 2 (2¾mm) knitting needles** for clothes
- Approx **½oz (10g) of polyester stuffing** for each bear
- **2 small black beads** for eyes
- **A tapestry or wool needle** for sewing up bear
- **Black or brown embroidery thread** for nose, mouth and claws
- **Forceps or tweezers** for turning and stuffing your bear (optional but very useful)
- **Safety pin or stitch holders** for working neckband of cardigan
- **4 tiny buttons or small beads and press fasteners** for cardigan
- A small **needle** for sewing buttons or press fastener and bead to cardigan

Height
Approximately 6 inches (15 cm).

Work in St st throughout unless otherwise stated.

Head and Body
Side A
With colour of choice, cast on 4 sts
Start with a K row
ROW 1—Inc in each st
ROW 2—P
ROW 3—Inc in each st (16 sts)
ROW 4—P
ROW 5—Inc 1 st at each end of row (18 sts)
St st 9 rows*
ROW 15—Dec 1 st at end of row (17 sts)
St st 9 rows
ROW 25—Dec 1 st at beg of row and every following alt row until 14 sts
ROW 30—P
ROW 31—(K2 tog, K2) 3 times, K2 tog (10 sts)
ROW 32—P
ROW 33—Dec 1 st at each end of row (8 sts)
ROW 34—P

The bears shown are knitted using Jaeger Matchmaker 4-ply Cream (662) and Soft Camel (718) with the dress in Cyclamen (694) and the cardigan in White (661) and Strawberry (633).

To shape head
ROW 35—Inc 1 st at each end of row (10 sts)
ROW 36—Inc 1 st at end of row
ROW 37—Inc 1 st at beg of row and each alt row until 15 sts
ROW 44—P
ROW 45—Dec 1 st at end of row (14 sts)
ROW 46—P
ROW 47—Cast off 4 sts, K to last 2 sts, K2 tog (9 sts)
ROW 48—Dec 1 st at each end of this and following row (5 sts)
Cast off remaining 5 sts, purling 2 sts tog at each end of row at the same time.

Head and Body
Side B
Work as side A to *
ROW 15—Dec 1 st at beg of row (17 sts)
St st 9 rows
ROW 25—Dec 1 st at end of row and every following alt row until 14 sts
ROW 30—P
ROW 31—(K2 tog, K2) 3 times, K2 tog (10 sts)
ROW 32—P
ROW 33—Dec 1 st at each end of row (8 sts)
ROW 34—P
ROW 35—K

To shape head

ROW 36—Inc 1 st at each end of row (10 sts)

ROW 37—Inc 1 st at end of row

ROW 38—Inc 1 st at beg of row and each alt row until 15 sts

ROW 45—K

ROW 46—Dec 1 st at end of row (14 sts)

ROW 47—K

ROW 48—Cast off 4 sts, P to lasts 2 sts, P2 tog (9 sts)

ROW 49—Dec 1 st at each end of this and following row (5 sts)

Cast off remaining 5 sts, knitting 2 sts tog at each end of row at the same time.

Head Gusset

To shape nose

With main colour cast on 2 st

ROW 1—Inc in each sts

ROW 2—P

ROW 3—Inc 1 st at each end of row (6 sts)

St st 7 rows

ROW 11—Inc 1 st at each end of row (8 sts)

St st 17 rows

ROW 29—Dec 1 st at each end of row and following 2 alt rows (2 sts)

P2 tog and fasten off.

Ears

make 2

With main colour cast on 7 sts work in G. st throughout:

K 2 rows

Dec 1 st at each end of next 2 rows (3 sts)

Cast off, leaving a long thread.

Right outer arm

make 1

With main colour, cast on 2 sts

Starting with a K row:

ROW 1—Inc in each st (4 sts)

ROW 2—P

ROW 3—Inc 1 st at beg and end of row (6 sts)

ROW 4—P

ROW 5—Inc 1 st at end of row (7 sts)

ROW 6—P

ROW 7—Dec 1 st at beg and Inc 1 st at end of row

ROW 8—P **

Rep last 2 rows twice

St st 6 rows

ROW 19—Inc 1 st at end of row (8 sts)

St st 9 rows

ROW 29—Dec 1 st at end of row (7 sts)

ROW 30—P

ROW 31—Dec 1 st at beg and end of row (5 sts)

ROW 32—P

Cast off, knitting 2 sts tog at beg and end of row at same time.

Left outer arm

make 1

With main colour, cast on 2 sts

Starting with a K row:

ROW 1—Inc in each st (4 sts)

ROW 2—P

ROW 3—Inc 1 st at beg and end of row (6 sts)

ROW 4—P

ROW 5—Inc 1 st at beg of row (7 sts)

ROW 6—P

ROW 7—Inc 1 st at beg and Dec 1 st at end of row

ROW 8—P **

Rep last 2 rows twice

St st 6 rows

ROW 19—Inc 1 st at beg of row (8 sts)

St st 9 rows

ROW 29 – Dec 1 st at beg of row (7 sts)

ROW 30 – P

ROW 31 – Dec 1 st at beg and end of row (5 sts)

ROW 32 – P

Cast off, knitting 2 sts tog at beg and end of row at the same time.

Inner arms

For reverse st st bears

make 2

Working in contrast colour, follow instructions as for right and left outer arms up to **

ROW 9—Rep row 7

ROW 10—Change to main colour and K 1 row (instead of purling)

ROW 11—Rep row 7

ROW 12—P

St st 6 rows, starting with a K row

Complete from row 19 to end.

(Don't forget to follow shaping for 1 left and 1 right arm)

If you want to make up one of these bears in stocking stitch (knit side facing), follow the instructions as for outer arms, starting with a contrast colour and changing to the main colour from **, then work to end.

Legs

make 2

Cast on 26 sts

ROW 1—K

ROW 2—Dec 1 st at each end of row and following alt row (22 sts)

ROW 5—K

ROW 6—Cast off 3 sts at beg of row

and following row

ROW 8—P

ROW 9—Inc 1 st at each end of row and following 6 th row (20 sts)

St st 6 rows

ROW 22—P2 tog, P6, P2 tog twice, P6, P2 tog

ROW 23—K

ROW 24—P2 tog, P4, P2 tog twice, P4, P2 tog

Cast off remaining 12 sts, slipping the first st.

Soles
make 2

In contrast colour, cast on 2 sts

Starting with a K row:

ROW 1—Inc in each st (4 sts)

ROW 2—P

ROW 3—Inc 1 st at beg and end of row (6 sts)

St st 10 rows

ROW 14—P2 tog, P2, P2 tog

ROW 15—K2 tog twice

ROW 16—P2 tog and finish off

To make up

Press all the pieces on the purl side with a warm iron, especially at the edges where they tend to curl in. Follow the instructions for making up *Annie & George* (see page 20) as these little bears are sewn up in exactly the same way.

Cardigan

Front and Back to armholes

With size 2 (2¾mm) needles and white, cast on 47 sts

Work 2 rows single rib

NEXT ROW—K2, join in pink and knit 1 st pink, 1 st white alternately across row to last 2 sts, K2 white

NEXT ROW—K2 white, then purl 1 st white, then 1 st pink alternately to last 2 sts, K2 white. Break off pink and continue in white

NEXT ROW—K

NEXT ROW—K2, purl to last 2 sts, K2

Rep last 2 rows twice

Right front

NEXT ROW—K10, K2 tog, turn and work on these sts only for now

NEXT ROW—P to last 2 sts, K2

NEXT ROW—K to last 2 sts, K2 tog

NEXT ROW—P to last 2 sts, K2

Rep the last 2 rows until 7 sts remain

To shape the neck

NEXT ROW—K2, and leave these sts on a safety pin, K2 tog, K1, K2 tog

NEXT ROW—P

NEXT ROW—K1, K2 tog

P2 tog and fasten off

Back

With right side facing, rejoin yarn,

NEXT ROW—K2 tog, K19, k2 tog, turn

NEXT ROW—P

Continue to dec as in last 2 rows until 9 sts remain, ending on a P row. Break yarn and leave sts on a holder.

Left Front

With right side facing rejoin yarn to remaining 12 sts

NEXT ROW—K2 tog, K to end

NEXT ROW—K2 P to end

Rep last 2 rows until 7 sts remain

To shape neck

NEXT ROW—K2 tog, K1, K2 tog, leave the last 2 sts on a safety pin for now,

turn and work on remaining sts

NEXT ROW—P

NEXT ROW—K2 tog, K1

NEXT ROW—P2 tog and fasten off

Sleeves
make 2

With size 2 (2¾mm) needles and white cast on 17sts

Work 2 rows single rib

Join in pink and St st 2 rows with alt sts of pink and white as in front and back, then continue in white

NEXT ROW—Inc 1 st at each end of row and following alt row (21 sts)

St st 5 rows

NEXT ROW—Dec 1 st at each end of row and every alt row until 7 sts

NEXT ROW—P to end and leave sts on a holder

71

To make up

With right sides facing, match up and sew raglan seams, placing the sts on holders onto one needle. With right sides facing, size 2 (2¾mm) needles and white, K across sts in following order: 2 sts from right border, pick up and K 3 sts along front neck, K 7 sts of right sleeve, 9 sts of back and 7 sts of left sleeve, pick up and K 3 sts along left neck and the 2 sts for left border. (33sts)

Rib 1 row

Cast off in rib.

Sew up all other seams, matching markers.

Sew on press fasteners and buttons as required.

Dress

To shape skirt

With size 2 (2¾mm) needles cast on 74 sts and G. st 2 rows

Starting with a P row St st 15 rows

NEXT ROW—K2 tog across row (37 sts)

Work 3 rows single rib

NEXT ROW—Cast off 11 sts, single K utnil there are 15 sts on the needle, cast off 11 sts

To make bib

With P side facing rejoin yarn to remaining 15 sts

NEXT ROW—K1, P1, K1, P9, K1, P1, K1

NEXT ROW—K1, P1, K11, P1, K1

Rep the last 2 rows 4 times ending on a K row

NEXT ROW—K1, P1, K11, P1, K1

Next row—K1, P1, K1, cast off next 9 sts, P1, K1

You should now have two sets of 3 sts for straps.

To make straps

Continue in moss st on first 3 sts until strap measures 2½ inches (6½cm). Leave the other 3 sts on a holder for now.

Cast off, leaving enough thread to sew end of strap to back of skirt

Rejoin yarn to remaining 3 sts and complete to match first strap.

Press the skirt of the dress well, avoiding the ribbed waistband. Sew up the back seam of the skirt. Cross the straps at the back and sew the ends to the waistband about ½ inch (1cm) either side of the seam.

Lily

Lily the panda has been made using a variation of the Elizabeth & Heidi instructions shown on pages 68–73.
She has a wider head, larger ears, and slightly larger arms.

Materials
- Approx 1oz each **fingering (30g 4-ply) yarn** in black and cream
- A pair of size **2 (2¾mm) knitting needles**
- 2 small (4mm) **black beads** or looped-back teddy eyes
- Strong **black thread**
- Approx ½oz (10g) of polyester stuffing
- A tapestry or wool needle
- **Black or brown embroidery thread** for nose mouth and claws

Height
Approximately 7 inches (18 cm).

Head and Body
Both sides
With cream yarn, follow the instructions for Elizabeth up to the end of row 15.
St st 7 rows
NEXT ROW—Join in black and knit 1 st black, 1 st cream alternately across row. Break cream yarn and continue in black
Work 1 row, then complete as for rest of head and body from row 25, changing back to cream yarn at beg of head shaping.

Head Gusset
In cream, cast on 3 sts
Starting with a K row, St st 2 rows
Inc 1 st at each end of next every following 4 th row until 11 sts
St st 7 rows

To shape nose
Dec 1 st at each end of next and following alt row (7 sts)
St st 7 rows
NEXT ROW—Dec 1 st at each end of row
Cast off, purling 2 sts tog at each end of row at same time.

Ears
make 2
With black, cast on 9 sts and work in G. st
K 2 rows
Dec 1 st at each end of next 2 rows
Cast off, slipping the first st and leaving a long thread.

Outside Arm
side A
make 1
With black, cast on 3 sts. Start with a K row
ROW 1—Inc 1 st at each end of row and following alt row
ROW 4—P
ROW 5—Inc 1 st at end of row (8 sts)
ROW 6—P
ROW 7—Dec 1 st at beg and Inc 1 st at end of row
ROW 8—P
ROW 9 AND 10—Rep the last 2 rows**
St st 6 rows
ROW 17—Inc 1 st at end of row
St st 11 rows (ending on a P row)
ROW 29—Dec 1 st at each end of row

and following alt row (5 sts)
Cast off, slipping the first st.

Outside Arm
Side B
make 1
With black, cast on 3 sts. Start with a K row
ROW 1—Inc 1 st at each end of row and following alt row
ROW 4—P
ROW 5—Inc 1 st at beg of row
ROW 6—P
ROW 7—Inc 1 st at beg and Dec 1 st at end of row
ROW 8—P
ROW 9 AND 10—Rep last 2 rows**
St st 6 rows
ROW 17—Inc 1 st at beg of row
Complete as for outside arm, side A

Inner Arms
Starting with cream colour, work as for outside arms to ** then change to black.

Legs and soles
Follow instructions for Elizabeth (page 71), using appropriate colours.

To make up
As for Elizabeth, but make a stocking stitch bear with reverse stocking stitch soles. Ensure the two colours are aligned at front and back of body when joining the seam. Darn in and snip off loose threads.

The bear shown is knitted in Matchmaker merino 4-ply soft Cream (376) and Black (383).

Oliver

This chubby little bear is very small and can be made up in a couple of evenings. If you can find a baby weight (3-ply) yarn in the right shade and use smaller needles, he will be tiny and can be classed as a miniature bear, being under 5 inches (12cm) high. You can of course make him larger by using thicker yarn and needles.

Materials
• 1oz fingering (30g 4-ply) yarn in the colour of your choice for bear and jacket
• 1 pair of **size US 2 (2¾mm) knitting needles** for bear and jacket
• **2 x 4mm black beads** or **loop-back eyes**
• **Strong black thread** for attaching beads or teddy eyes
• **Approx ½oz (10g) of polyester stuffing**
• **Black or brown embroidery thread** for nose, mouth and claws
• **2 press fasteners** or small **buttons, thread and sewing needle** for jacket
• **Forceps or tweezers** (optional)

The bear shown is knitted using leftover yarn. He could be made using Patons Diploma fingering weight (4-ply) yarn in Natural (4283) and Denim (4136).

Height
Approximately 6 inches (15cm).

Head
Side A
make 1
Cast on 10 sts Start with a K row
ROW 1—Inc 1 st at each end of row
ROW 2—P
ROW 3—Inc 1 st at beg of row and each following alt row until 16 sts
ROW 10—P
ROW 11—Cast off 6 sts at beg of row. Place marker at last cast off st.
ROW 12—P
ROW 13—K
ROW 14—Dec 1 st at each end of this and following row
Cast off remaining 6 sts, purling 2 sts tog at each end of row at same time.

Head
Side B
make 1
Cast on 10 sts Start with a P row
ROW 1—Inc 1 st at each end of row
ROW 2—K
ROW 3—Inc 1 st at beg of row and each following alt row until 16 sts
ROW 10—K
ROW 11—Cast off 6 sts at beg of row Place marker at last cast off st.
ROW 12—K
ROW 13—P
ROW 14—Dec 1 st at each end of this and following row

Cast off remaining 6 sts, knitting 2 sts tog at each end of row at same time.

Head gusset
Starting at back of neck
Cast on 3 sts
ROW 1—P
Inc 1 st at each end of next and every 4 th row until 9 sts
St st 13 rows (ending on a P row
To shape nose
Dec 1 st at each end of next 2 rows (5 sts) Place marker at each end of last row
St st 5 rows
Cast off, purling 2 sts tog at each end of row at same time.

Ears
Cast on 7 sts and G. st 4 rows
NEXT ROW—K2 tog at each end of row
Cast off, knitting 2 sts tog at each end of row at same time.

Body Front
make 1
To shape bottom and tummy
Cast on 4 sts Start with a K row
ROW 1—Inc in each st (8 sts)
ROW 2—P
ROW 3—Inc in each st (16 sts)
ROW 4—P
ROW 5—K7, Inc in next 2 sts, K7 **
ROW 6—P
ROW 7—K8, Inc in next 2 sts, K8 (20 sts)

ROW 8—P
ROW 9—K9, Inc in next 2 sts, K9
ROW 10—P
ROW 11—K10, Inc in next 2 sts, K10
(24 sts)
St st 13 rows (ending on a P row)

To shape chest

ROW 25—K2 tog, K8, K2 tog twice, K8, K2 tog
ROW 26—P
ROW 27—K8, K2 tog twice, K8
ROW 28—P
ROW 29—K2 tog, K5, K2 tog twice, K5, K2 tog (14 sts)
ROW 30—P
ROW 31—K2 tog, K3, K2 tog twice, K3, K2 tog (10 sts)
Cast off in P

Body Back
make 1
Work as front up to ** (18 sts)
St st 9 rows

To shape lower back

ROW 15—K7, K2 tog twice, K7
St st 3 rows
ROW 19—K7, Inc in next 2 sts, K7
St st 7 rows
ROW 27—K2 tog, K5, K2 tog twice, K5, K2 tog
ROW 28—P
ROW 29—K5, K2 tog twice, K5
ROW 30—P
ROW 31—K2 tog, K2, K2 tog twice, K2, K2 tog (8 sts)
Cast off in P

Arms
make 2
To shape paws

Cast on 3 sts Start with a K row
ROW 1—Inc in each st
ROW 2—P
ROW 3—Inc 1, K1, Inc in next 2 sts, K1, Inc 1 (10 sts)
ROW 4—P
ROW 5—Inc 1 st at each end of row
ROW 6—P
ROW 7—Inc 1, K3, K2 tog twice, K3, Inc 1
ROW 8—P
Rep last 2 rows once
St st 4 rows
ROW 15—Inc 1 st at each end of row (14 sts)
St st 7 rows
ROW 23—Dec 1 st at each end of row
ROW 24—P
ROW 25—K2 tog, K2, K2 tog twice, K2, K2 tog
Cast off in P, slipping the first st

Legs
make 2
Cast on 22 sts Start with a K row
St st 2 rows
ROW 3—Dec 1 st at each end of this and following row (18 sts)
ROW 5—K2 tog, K6, K2 tog, K6, K2 tog
ROW 6—Dec 1 st at each end of row
ROW 7—Inc 1, K5, Inc 1, K5, Inc 1 (16 sts)
St st 9 rows
ROW 17—K2 tog, K4, K2 tog twice, K4, K2 tog
ROW 18—P
Cast off knitting 2 sts tog at each end of row at same time

Soles
Cast on 3 sts Start with a K row
ROW 1—Inc 1 st at each end of row (5 sts)
St st 9 rows
ROW 11—K2 tog, K1, K2 tog
Cast off in P, slipping the first st

To make up
The purl side is the right side of work.

Press all the pieces well, especially at the edges where they tend to curl in. Using a tiny backstitch and with purl sides together, join front and back body pieces together all round from back neck to front neck. Turn out and stuff carefully through neck opening but do not close, leave to one side for now. Sew up the head side pieces from tip of nose to chin. Insert the head gusset, matching markers (these are the approximate eye positions) and stuff the head, moulding and shaping as you go along and making sure the nose area is well stuffed first. Leave the bottom (neck) edge open. Sew the head to the body, matching neck edges and adding a bit more stuffing as you go along. Tie a length of yarn around the neck and pull up, not too tightly. Fasten off and sink the ends into the bear out of sight. Sew up, stuff and thread-joint the limbs to the body. Sew the ears to the head, quite far back and with a pronounced curve.

Sink the bead eyes into place (see General Instructions on page 13), or sew one or two tiny stitches with black or brown embroidery thread. Embroider a small nose, mouth and claws.

Jacket

Work in G. st throughout.

Right Front

Cast on 10 sts
Row 1—Inc 1 st at beg of row
K 7 rows straight, ending at front edge
To shape underarm edge
Row 9—Inc 1 st at the end of row
Row 10—Inc 1 st at beg of row
Row 11—Rep row 9 (14 sts)
K 5 rows, ending at front edge
To shape front
Row 17—K1, K2 tog, K to end
K 3 rows
Rep last 4 rows twice
Cast off remaining 11 sts

Left Front

Cast on 10 sts
Row 1—Inc 1 st at end of row
K 7 rows straight, ending at side edge
To shape underarm edge
Row 9—Inc 1 st at beg of row
Row 10—Inc 1 st at end of row
Row 11—Rep row 9
K 5 rows, ending at side edge
To shape front
Row 17—K to last 3 sts, K2 tog, K1
K 3 rows
Rep last 4 rows twice
Cast off remaining 11 sts

Back

Cast on 20 sts
K 8 rows straight
To shape underarm edge
Row 9—Inc 1 st at each end of this
and following 2 rows (26 sts)

K 14 rows straight

To shape back neck

Row 26—K11, cast off the next 4 sts,
K to end
For right shoulder
NEXT ROW—Dec 1 st at end of row
NEXT ROW—K
Cast off
For left shoulder
NEXT ROW—Rejoin yarn to neck edge
and Dec 1 st at beg of row
NEXT ROW—K
Cast off

To make up

Do not press. Join shoulder and
underarm seams. Dress the bear,
overlap the jacket fronts slightly and
sew on the buttons through both
layers. If you want the jacket to undo,
sew the buttons on one side and press
fasteners on the back to correspond
with the buttons.

Molly, Toby & Jake

These miniature bears are quick and easy to knit although they are fiddly to make up because of the small pieces—a pair of tweezers will help you turn and stuff them. They are very sweet and are ideal as collectors' bears, mascots or pocket-sized friends. They are not suitable for young children because of their size and the tiny bead eyes.

Materials:
- Approx **1oz fingering (30g 4-ply) yarn** in the colour of your choice for each bear
- Approx **1oz fingering (30g 4-ply) yarn** in the colour of your choice for the vest (waistcoat)
- A pair of **US 1 (2¼ mm) knitting needles**
- Small **black beads** for eyes
- **Black thread and needle for attaching eyes**
- Approx **¼oz (5g) of polyester stuffing** for each bear
- A **tapestry or wool needle** for sewing up the bears
- **Black or brown embroidery thread** for nose, mouth and claws
- **Forceps or tweezers** for turning and stuffing bears (optional)

The bears shown are knitted in acrylic yarn. A yarn with only a small percentage of wool is most suitable for these tiny bears.

Height
Approximately 4 inches (10 cm).

Work in St st throughout unless otherwise stated. Pieces will then be sewn up purl sides together to give a reverse St st bear.

Body and Head
—all one piece up to neck
Cast on 8 sts Start with a K row
ROW 1—Inc in each st (16 sts)
ROW 2—P
ROW 3—Inc 1, K6, Inc in next 2 sts, K6, Inc 1 (20 sts)
ROW 4—P
ROW 5—Inc 1, K8, Inc in next 2 sts, K8, Inc 1 (24 sts)
ROW 6—P
ROW 7—K11, Inc in next 2 sts, K11 (26 sts)
St st 3 rows

To shape back
ROW 11—Dec 1 st at beg and end of row
St st 5 rows
ROW 17—Inc 1 st at beg and end of row
ROW 18—P
ROW 19—K11, K2 tog twice, K11 (24 sts)
ROW 20—P
ROW 21—K2 tog, K8, K2 tog twice, K8, K2 tog
ROW 22—P
ROW 23—(K2 tog, K2) twice, K2 tog

twice, (K2, K2 tog) twice (14 sts)
ROW 24—P2 tog, P3, P2 tog twice, P3, P2 tog
ROW 25—K5, turn and work on these sts only for now

To shape first side of head
ROW 26—Inc 1 st at beg and end of row (7 sts)
ROW 27—Inc 1 st at end of row
ROW 28—Inc 1 st at beg of row and following 2 alt rows (11 sts)
ROW 33—K

To shape nose
ROW 34—Cast off 4 sts, P to last 2 sts, P2 tog (6 sts)
ROW 35—K
ROW 36—P2 tog, P2, P2 tog
Cast off remaining 4 sts, slipping the first st

To shape second side of head
With K side facing, rejoin yarn to remaining 5 sts
ROW 25—Inc 1 st at beg and end of row (7 sts)
ROW 26—Inc 1 st at end of row
ROW 27—Inc 1 st at beg of row and following 2 alt rows (11 sts)
ROW 32—P

To shape nose
ROW 33—Cast off 4 sts, K to last 2 sts, K2 tog (6 sts)
ROW 34—P

ROW 35—K2 tog, K2, K2 tog
Cast off, slipping the first st

Head Gusset
Make 1
Starting at nose
Cast on 3 sts, leaving a longish thread
to identify which is the nose end
when sewing up
Start with a K row
St st 4 rows
ROW 5—Inc 1 st at beg and end of row
and following alt row (7 sts).
St st 7 rows (ending on a P row)
ROW 15—(K1, K2 tog) twice, K1
St st 3 rows
ROW 19—K2 tog, K1, K2 tog
ROW 20—P
Cast off last 3 sts, slipping the first st
and leaving a short thread.

Ears
make 2
Cast on 6 sts, working in G. st:
K 2 rows
NEXT ROW—K 2 tog, K2, K2 tog
K2 tog twice, pass 1 st over the other
and finish off, leaving a long thread

Arms
make 2
Starting at paw
Cast on 3 sts
ROW 1—Inc in each st (6 sts)
ROW 2—P
ROW 3—Inc 1, K1, Inc in next 2 sts,
K1, Inc 1 (10 sts)
ROW 4—P
ROW 5—Inc 1, K2, K2 tog twice, K2,
Inc 1
ROW 6—P
ROW 7—Rep row 5

St st 5 rows
ROW 13—Inc 1, K to last 2 sts, Inc 1,
K1 (12 sts)
St st 7 rows
ROW 21—K2 tog, K2, K2 tog twice,
K2, K2 tog (8 sts)
ROW 22—P
ROW 23—(K2 tog, K1) twice, K2 tog
Cast off, slipping the first st

Legs
make 2
Cast on 18 sts Start with a K row
St st 3 rows

To shape toes
ROW 4—Dec 1 st st at beg and end
of row
ROW 5—Cast off 3 sts at beg of row, K
to last 3 sts, cast off 3 sts (10 sts) and
break yarn.
ROW 6—With wrong side facing, rejoin
yarn and P
ROW 7—Inc 1 st at beg and end of row
and following alt row (14 sts)
St st 7 rows
ROW 17—K2 tog, K3, K2 tog twice,
K3, K2 tog
ROW 18—P
ROW 19—K2 tog, K1, K2 tog twice,
K1, K2 tog
Cast off in P

Soles
make 2
Cast on 2 sts Start with a K row
ROW 1—Inc in each st (4 sts)
St st 7 rows
ROW 9—K2 tog twice
Cast off

To make up
Press all pieces lightly. Darn in and
trim all loose ends except the long
thread at the top of the ears and at
the nose end of the gusset.

For a teddy in reverse st st, match
all pieces purl sides together to
sew up.

To sew pieces together, pinch the
seams together between your finger
and thumb of one hand. You could
pin the pieces together first if you
want to, but I find that pins get in
the way on such a small bear. Use
an oversew stitch and sew very
small stitches quite close together,
checking frequently that the seams
are still aligned. Use a ladderstitch
to close gaps in seams after stuffing.

Head and Body
With P sides together sew up the
seam from front neck (a) to nose (b)
shown on diagram, right.

Sew the head gusset to both sides
of the head from the nose (b) to the
back of the head (c), adjusting to fit
(you may need to use a couple of
pins here). The long thread you left
when knitting the gusset will identify
which is the nose end.

Sew about ½ inch (1cm) down the
shoulders and back from (c) to (d).

And from the lower back (e) to the
bottom (f).

You should now have a gap in the
back for turning and stuffing.

Turn right side out and stuff
carefully, filling out the nose first and
moulding into shape as you go, be
careful not to overstuff and stretch
the knitting. Close the back opening

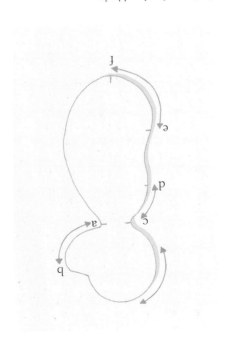

Sewing up head and body.

using ladderstitch. Tie a piece of the same colour yarn around the neck and pull firmly to define the neck and shoulders. Tie a knot and sink the ends of the thread into the body out of sight.

Ears

Sew in and trim off the shorter cast on thread. Thread the long cast off thread at the top of an ear onto your needle. Weave this thread through the sts at one side of the ear down to the base, and pull slightly to "round off" the top of the ear, then take a couple of sts to anchor the thread.

Repeat with the other ear, then pin and sew the ears to head. It's a good idea to experiment with the position of the ears before you sew them. I usually place them almost at the back of the head and over the gusset line.

Eyes

As a collector's bear or mascot for an adult, you can use tiny black beads for the eyes, and they do look much more effective. For how to insert bead eyes see the General Instructions on page 13.

Nose and Mouth

Using two strands of embroidery thread, sew between six and eight stitches for the nose, and either two or three single stitches for the mouth shape of choice.

Arms

Fold each arm lengthways, P sides together, pin and sew up the seams leaving a small gap at the front for turning and stuffing. Turn out and stuff carefully, using very small amounts of stuffing at a time, and only lightly stuff the tops of the arms. Check that both arms match each other in size then sew up the gap in the seams. Sew three tiny claws to each paw if you wish.

Legs

Fold each leg in half lengthways, P sides together. Pin and sew, leaving the bottom edges open and a small gap at the front for turning and stuffing. Pin, adjust and sew the soles to the feet. Turn out and stuff carefully, using very small amounts of stuffing at a time. Check that each leg matches the other in size, then sew up the gap in the seams using ladderstitch.

Attaching the Limbs

These little bears are thread-jointed. For how to do this, see the General Instructions on page 13.

Vest (waistcoat)

Worked in one piece to armholes

With chosen colour and working in G. st. throughout:

Cast on 30 sts

Inc 1 st at each end of next and following alt row (34 sts)

K 7 rows straight

NEXT ROW—K7, cast off 3 sts, K until there are 14 sts on the needle, cast off 3 sts, K to end

There should now be 7 sts for each front and 14 sts for the back.

Left side

working on first 7 sts only

NEXT ROW—K

NEXT ROW—K2, K2 tog, K2, K2 tog, K1

K 3 rows

NEXT ROW—K2, K2 tog, K1

K 3 rows

NEXT ROW—K1, K2 tog, K1

K 3 rows

Cast off

Back

With wrong side facing, rejoin yarn to back 14 sts

NEXT ROW—K

NEXT ROW—Dec 1 st at each end of row

K 9 rows straight

To shape shoulders

NEXT ROW—K4, cast off next 4 sts, K to end
NEXT ROW—K2, K2 tog
Cast off

Next shoulder

Rejoin yarn to neck edge of last 4 sts
NEXT ROW—K2 tog, K2
Cast off

Right Side

With wrong side facing, rejoin yarn to remaining sts
NEXT ROW—K
NEXT ROW—K1, K2 tog, K2, K2 tog
K 3 rows
NEXT ROW—K1, K2 tog, K2
K3 rows
NEXT ROW—K1, K2 tog, K1
K 3 rows
Cast off

Do not press. Join shoulder seams.

Add lace and ribbons as desired.

A miniature bear shown in white.

Old Bears

Old bears have a great charm and are always popular. If you haven't got an old bear, the next best thing is to make one. During his lifetime, Old Ted will have loosened up and lost a few claws. His ears and seams will be worn and probably need restitching. For your heirloom, you will need to recreate this look.

Materials
- Approx **1oz (30g)** of baby weight or fingering (3- or 4-ply) tweed or recycled yarn
- A pair of **US 1 (2¼mm) knitting needles**
- Approx **½oz (10g)** of polyester **stuffing**
- 4 old **shirt buttons**
- Strong **thread** to sew on eyes and buttons
- 1 pair of **¼ inch (3mm) beads** or looped-back teddy eyes
- **Brown embroidery thread** for nose, mouth and claws
- 1 teaspoon of lead pellets

William

William is made using the *Elizabeth & Heidi* pattern on pages 68–73. The bear shown was made using a second-hand batch of fingering (4-ply) yarn. His "joints" are old shirt buttons. Any thin yarn you may have lying around at home would be ideal.

A small bag of lead pellets in William's tummy gives him some weight to flop about (this is not recommended for a child's bear). You can buy a bag of this from hobby and craft stores or teddy bear fairs. Make a small bag to hold the pellets by knitting an oblong of 12 sts by 24 rows. Fold in half to form a bag and sew up, leaving one side open. Add the pellets and close the seam. Stuff the head firmly, then place the pellet bag into the body and stuff around it. Stuff the tops of the arms and legs and around the neck area loosely. To join on the limbs, follow the General Instructions for thread-jointing on page 13, incorporating the buttons onto the outside of the limbs at the same time. Sew on the ears (don't be too fussy about exact placement) and then the eyes, nose and mouth. The eyes are deliberately smaller than Elizabeth's to give an older look.

Sew three claws onto the paws, missing out one or two here and there. Using two strands of the embroidery thread, make some obvious stitching along a couple of the seams. You could add a tiny patch of fabric, or darn one.

Charlie

Charlie was made using the instructions for Robert (see pages 26–31) with some slight alterations. I used an old, recycled fingering (4-ply) weight cotton yarn, size 2 (2¼mm) knitting needles and ½ inch (12mm) safety eyes.

Knit up all the pieces as for Robert but with about four rows less in the arm length. His contrast paw pads are also a bit shorter, so do one less repeat of the two paw shaping rows and make it up with the main colour. Don't be too fussy when fixing the safety eyes in position or when stuffing him, on this occasion it doesn't matter if your knitting is a bit stretched in places and saggy in others. His ears would also be a bit out of shape by now, so don't sew them on too carefully either. I have thread-jointed Charlie but he would work with button joints. To make his eyes look older they have been scratched very slightly with a piece of sandpaper. If you try this be careful not to overdo it as they do mark easily. He has no claws as this adds to a feeling of old age and wear and tear.

Scarf

With whatever fingering (4-ply) yarns you have, cast on 15 sts and work in St st until scarf measures about 18 inches (45 cm) or length required. Work either 2 or 4 rows randomly of each colour so that you always finish on a P row, snipping off and tying the threads regularly as you go along, otherwise they will start to come undone before you have finished the scarf. When finished, fold lengthways, right sides together and sew up along the side edges. Fasten a large safety pin to one short edge and use this to pull the scarf the right way out. Do not sew up the

ends yet. To fringe the scarf, follow the instructions given for Thomas's scarf (see page 42), pushing your crochet hook through the stitches of both layers of scarf and using longer lengths of yarn (just over double the required finished length). Trim to neaten. If you don't want a fringe, sew the two ends closed.

Douglas

Materials
- Approx **2oz worsted (50g D/K) yarn** for bear and clothes.
- Sizes **US 2 and 3 (3mm and 3¼mm) knitting needles**
- 3 white **shirt buttons or press fasteners**
- Grey or black **embroidery thread** for nose and mouth
- **1oz (30g) polyester stuffing**
- A **tapestry or wool needle**
- **2 tiny buttons** or ¼ inch **(5mm) beads** for eyes
- **Safety pins or holders** for cardigan

To make the bear

Follow the instructions for *Bertie & Bruce* (see pages 62–67) except for ears, which are as follows:

From left to right: Douglas, Charlie and William. Douglas is knitted in Jaeger luxury tweed Pebble (820) and Jaeger Matchmaker D/K Clarice (876). Charlie and William are made from recycled yarns.

Ears
make 2

Cast on 9 sts and G, st 3 rows
Dec 1 st at each end of row and following alt row
Cast off, knitting 2 sts at each end of row at same time.

To make up

As with the other two bears, do not be too fussy about sewing up, an oversew st would be better on this occasion. Stuff loosely. Sew eyes in place. Stitch nose and mouth with the grey thread (how much you leave out is up to you). Thread-joint loosely.

Cardigan

As this cardigan is for an "old" bear I have used worsted (D/K) yarn as most clothes for old bears would have been made from leftover yarn and old shirt buttons. The buttonholes are optional—you can use press fasteners with smaller buttons on the fronts instead. This cardigan will also fit Thomas if he is knitted in fingering (4-ply) yarn.

The back and fronts are knitted in one piece up to the armholes then finished off separately.

Back and Fronts
Worked in one piece

With size US 2 (3mm) needles, cast on 60 sts and work in single rib and G. st as follows:
ROW 1—K3, rib to last 3 sts, K3
ROW 2—Rep last row
ROW 3—(Buttonhole row)—K3, rib to last 4 sts, K2 tog, yfwd, K2
ROW 4—Rep row 1

With size US 3 (3¼mm) needles and starting with a K row, St st 10 rows, keeping the first and last 3 sts K in every row for front borders.

To shape armholes and work 2nd buttonhole

NEXT ROW—K13, cast off next 6 sts, K until there are 22 sts on the needle for the back, cast off the next 6 sts, K to last 4 sts, K2 tog, yfwd, K2. You should now have 13 sts for each side and 22 sts for the back. The back and fronts are now worked separately, you can keep all the pieces on your needle as you work or place them on a safety pin for now.

Left Front

NEXT ROW—K3, P to end
NEXT ROW—K1, Sl 1, K1, psso, K to end
NEXT ROW—K3, P to end
Continue to Dec at armhole edge in every K row until 9 sts remain, ending on a K row.

To shape front

NEXT ROW—K3, leave these sts on a safety pin for now, P to end
NEXT ROW—K1, Sl 1, K1, psso, K1, K2 tog
NEXT ROW—P
NEXT ROW—K1, Sl 1, K1, psso, K1
NEXT ROW—P
NEXT ROW—K1, Sl 1, K1, psso
P2 tog and fasten off

Back

With P side facing, rejoin yarn to the 22 sts for the back and P 1 row
NEXT ROW—K1, Sl 1, K1, psso, K to

NEXT ROW—K2 tog, K1
P2 tog and fasten off

Sleeves

With size US 2 (2¾mm) needles, cast on 22 sts and work in a single rib for 3 rows
Change to size 3 (3¼mm) needles and St st 8 rows, Inc 1 st at each end of 3 rd row (24 sts)

To shape armholes

Cast off 3 sts at beginning of next 2 rows
NEXT ROW—K1, Sl 1, K1, psso, K to last 3 sts, K2 tog, K1
NEXT ROW—P
Continue to Dec in this way until 6 sts remain, ending on a P row, leave sts on a holder for now.

To make up

Join sleeve under arm seams then fit in sleeves and join raglan seams.
With size US 2 (2¾mm) needles and right sides facing, slip the 3 sts of right front onto needle, pick up and K 7 sts up right side of neck, K across 6 sts of right sleeve, 8 sts of back, 6 sts of left sleeve, then pick up and K 7 sts down left side of neck and K3 sts on left front (40 sts).

Neck border

NEXT ROW—K3, rib to last 3 sts, K3
Work 3 more rows in rib with G. st front borders, making another buttonhole in the first row as follows:
K3, rib to last 4 sts, K2 tog, yfwd, K2
Cast off in rib.
Tidy up loose threads and sew on buttons.

last 3 sts, K2 tog, K1
NEXT ROW—P
Rep last 2 rows until 8 sts remain and leave on a holder or safety pin for now.

Right Front

With P side facing, rejoin yarn to remaining 13 sts
NEXT ROW—P to last 3 sts, K3
NEXT ROW—K to last 3 sts, K2 tog, K1

Continue to Dec in this way until 9 sts remain, ending at front edge

To shape front

NEXT ROW—K3, leave these sts on a safety pin for now, K to last 3 sts, K2 tog, K1
NEXT ROW—P
NEXT ROW—K2 tog twice, K1
NEXT ROW—P

A Recycled Bear

This little cutie is knitted using the Snowflake pattern shown on pages 90–92 in recycled double knitting yarn with size US 3 (3mm) needles. Teddy bears aren't fussy and the most handsome creations can be made from oddments left over from other projects.

Nowadays, very few people bother to reknit yarn from handknitted garments. This is a shame because there is something very satisfying about creating a new character from something that would otherwise have been thrown away.

Experiment with different colours—don't feel that you must stick rigidly to the traditional bear colours. Bears made in a variety of colours are shown on pages 93–95. Hopefully these will inspire you to experiment and make your own versions of the teddies in this book.

Most yarns, especially wool, can be reconditioned for reknitting quite easily. Whether you decide to recycle for economy reasons or just because "it's a shame to waste it", recycled yarn can make a very nice teddy bear. Knitwear for recycling must be in good condition and not felted or matted. Brushed or hairy yarns will probably not be suitable as they will be too difficult to undo.

First unpick all the seams—this will be easier if they have been oversewn instead of backstitched. Take your time unpicking so that you don't keep breaking the stitches or you will end up with a lot of small balls of yarn and have to keep joining on lengths as you knit up your bear. When undoing the knitted pieces you can either wind the yarn into

Lovable bears like this can be made using old scraps of yarn you already have at home.

balls as you go along or let it pile up loosely (undisturbed) and wind it into skeins at intervals as it builds up. When the yarn is unravelled it will be very crinkly. The best way to get it back to a condition that is good enough to knit with is to wash it.

The yarn should be in skeins for washing. When you have wound a manageable sized skein (about 1oz or 20–30g), tie it in a couple of places with a short length of a differently coloured yarn and knot tightly. Dilute some washing powder or liquid in lukewarm water and gently immerse and lift the skeins in and out of the water a few times. Rinse in clean water, then lay a couple of skeins at a time onto a small towel. Roll up fairly tightly, fold over into a packet and place in the spin drier for a short spin. To dry fully, fold the skeins over a clothes dryer. When they are completely dry wind them into balls which should iron out most of the rest of the crinkles. To prevent the yarn tangling as you wind it up, try wrapping the skein around a chair back, a piece of cardboard or somebody's hands!

Snowflake

Although at first glance the pattern looks a bit complicated, this little bear is quite simple and very quick to knit up. The body and head are all one piece, with a centre seam and no head gusset to insert. The arms and legs are also one piece each and both arms are the same.

Materials

- Approx **2oz (50g)** mohair yarn in the colour of your choice
- **1 pair of US 3 (3mm)** knitting needles
- Approx **½oz (10g)** of polyester stuffing
- A tapestry or wool needle
- **Small beads** or looped-back teddy eyes
- **Strong black thread** for attaching bead or teddy eyes
- **Black or brown embroidery thread** for nose, mouth and claws
- **Ribbon** to tie round bear's neck

The bear shown is knitted in Jaeger Mohair Art in Frost (600).

Height

Approximately 7¼ inches (18cm).

Work in St st throughout except for the ears, which are worked in G. st. Start all pieces with a K row.

Body and Head
all 1 piece

Starting at base
Cast on 11 sts
ROW 1—(Inc 1, K1) 5 times, Inc 1 (17 sts)
ROW 2—P
ROW 3—Inc in each st (34 sts)
Starting with a P row, St st 19 rows

To shape shoulders

ROW 23—K7, K2 tog twice, K12, K2 tog twice, K7 (30 sts)
St st 3 rows
ROW 27—K6, K2 tog twice, K10, K2 tog twice, K6 (26 sts)
ROW 28—P2 tog, P5, P2 tog, P8, P2 tog, P5, P2 tog (22 sts)
St st 2 rows

To shape left side of head

ROW 1—K5, Inc in next 2 sts, K3, Inc 1 (14 sts), now turn and work on these sts only for now
ROW 2—Inc 1, P6, Inc 1, P to end (16 sts)
ROW 3—K8, Inc 1, K6, Inc 1 (18 sts)
ROW 4—P
ROW 5—K7, Inc 1, K to end (19 sts)

St st 4 rows
ROW 10—P2 tog, P to end
ROW 11—K to last 2 sts, K2 tog
ROW 12—P2 tog, P6, P2 tog, P to end (15 sts)
ROW 13—K6, K2 tog, K5, K2 tog (13 sts)
ROW 14—P
ROW 15—K5, K2 tog twice, K4 (11 sts)
ROW 16—P2 tog, P1, P2 tog twice, P to end (8 sts)
ROW 17—(K2 tog, K2) twice (6 sts)
ROW 18—P3 tog twice, pass 1 st over the other and finish off

To shape right side of head

With right side of work facing, rejoin yarn to complete head
ROW 1—Inc 1, K3, Inc in next 2 sts, K to end (14 sts)
ROW 2—P6, Inc 1, P6, Inc 1 (16 sts)
ROW 3—Inc 1, K6, Inc 1, K to end (18 sts)
ROW 4—P
ROW 5—K10, Inc 1, K to end (19 sts)
St st 4 rows
ROW 10—P to last 2 sts, P2 tog
ROW 11—K2 tog, K to end
ROW 12—P7, P2 tog, P to last 2 sts, P2 tog (15 sts)
ROW 13—K2 tog, K5, K2 tog, K to end (13 sts)
ROW 14—P
ROW 15—K4, K2 tog twice, K5
ROW 16—P4, P2 tog twice, P1, P2 tog

(8 sts)

ROW 17—(K2 tog, K2) twice (6 sts)

ROW 18—P3 tog twice, pass 1 st over the other and finish off

Ears
make 2

Work in G. st throughout.

Cast on 9 sts

K 2 rows

Dec 1 st at each end of next 2 rows (5 sts)

Cast off, slipping the first st and leaving a long thread

Arms
make 2

Starting at paw

Cast on 4 sts

ROW 1—Inc in each st (8 sts)

ROW 2—P

ROW 3—Inc 1, K2, Inc in next 2 sts, K2, Inc 1 (12 sts)

ROW 4—P

ROW 5—Inc 1 st at each end of row (14 sts)

ROW 6—P

ROW 7—Inc 1, K4, K2 tog twice, K4, Inc 1

ROW 8—P

Rep last 2 rows

St st 4 rows

ROW 15—Inc 1 st at each end of row (16 sts)

St st 7 rows

ROW 23—Dec 1 st at each end of row

ROW 24—P

ROW 25—K2 tog, K3, K2 tog twice, K3, K2 tog (10 sts)

ROW 26—P

Cast off remaining sts, knitting 2 tog at each end of row and the middle of

the row at the same time

Legs
make 2

Cast on 24 sts

St st 3 rows

ROW 4—Dec 1 st at each end of row and following alt row (20 sts)

ROW 7—K

Cast off 3 sts at beg of next 2 rows (14 sts)

ROW 10—P

ROW 11—Inc 1 st at each end of row and following 4 th row (18 sts)

St st 5 rows

ROW 21—(K2 tog, K6) twice, K2 tog (15 sts)

ROW 22—P

ROW 23—K2 tog, K4, Sl 1, K2 tog, psso, K4, K2 tog (11 sts)

Cast off, slipping the first st

To make up
Head and Body

With K sides together and starting at the front of the neck, match up, pin and sew the two head sides, then continue down the back of the head and neck to the bottom of the bear, leaving a small gap in the back seam for turning and stuffing. Turn right side out and stuff firmly and carefully, filling out the nose area first and moulding into shape as you go. Close the gap in the seam, then tie a piece of the same coloured yarn around the neck and pull fairly tightly to further define the head and shoulders.

Ears

Sew in and trim off the shorter cast on thread. Thread the longer thread

onto the needle; weave it in along the edge of the ear down to the corner and pull slightly to give a nice rounded shape. Take a couple of sts to anchor the thread and use the rest to sew the ears to the head. Pin and sew the ears about ½ inch (1cm) in from the back of the head and about ½ inch (1cm) apart, curving the edges in slightly.

Arms and Legs

Pin and sew up the legs, K sides together, leaving a small gap as in the body for turning and stuffing. Turn out and stuff firmly, filling out the feet first. Close the gap in the seam. Pin and sew up each arm in the same way as the legs. Turn out and stuff carefully, not as firmly as the head, body and legs. Close the gap in the seam.

Attaching Limbs

The limbs are attached by thread-jointing—see General Instructions on page 13.

Eyes

Instructions for attaching bead or looped-back teddy eyes, or sewing eyes with embroidery thread are given on page 13.

Nose, Mouth and Claws

Using black or brown embroidery thread, stitch a mouth and nose of your choice following instructions as for one of the smaller bears such as Annie or George on pages 17–21. See General Instructions on page 13 for how to make claws.

Using Different Colours

Teddy bears aren't fussy and the most handsome creations can be made from scraps of yarn which you may have lying around the house from other projects. This is your chance to experiment!

Although it is nice to work with all the great new yarns available today, it shouldn't put you off if you cannot afford them or cannot get hold of them. Most well-known bear makers produce bears in unusual colours—blue bears in particular have been around for some time and many bear collectors have one in their collection.

Red Bear

Follow instructions for *Robert* (pages 26–31) using worsted (D/K) yarn.

Light blue bear

Follow instructions for *Bertie & Bruce* (pages 62–67) with worsted (D\K) yarn of your choice.

Lilac bear with baby

Follow instructions for *Ralph* (pages 56–59), using a worsted (D\K) knitting yarn for Mother bear and fingering (4-py yarn) and the miniature bear pattern for the baby.

Red, white and blue bear

Follow instructions for a miniature bear (pages 80–84), using colours as shown.

Jester Bear

Follow the instructions for *Annie & George* (pages 16–21) with the following changes:

Legs

Work in gold colour to row 9, changing red/blue in row 10

Arms

As this bear is sewn up with the knit sides facing, instructions for inside arms are not required. Make 1 pair of outside arms in blue and 1 in red as follows: Work in gold to row 10, changing to red/blue at**

Body and head

Work one side of the body red and one side blue up to row 33, changing to gold in row 34 Sew up this bear with right sides together. Sew on beads/buttons

Ruffle

Gather a piece of 1 inch (2½ inch) ribbon and sew in place.

Hat

Cast on 30 sts and K 3 rows Starting with a K row, St st 8 rows straight Next row—K2 tog, K11, K2 tog, turn and work on these sts only for now
NEXT ROW—Purl
Dec 1 st at each end of next and every following alt row until 5 sts
NEXT ROW—Purl
Cut yarn, leaving a length of about

4 inches (10cm), thread onto a needle and then run thread through sts and pull up tightly

With right side facing, rejoing yarn to remaining 15 sts

NEXT ROW—K2 tog, K11, K2 tog

NEXT ROW—Purl

Complete as first side

With right sides tog, sew up side seams, turn up hat rim and sew on pompoms. Sew hat to head.

Pompoms

Thread a wool needle with about a metre length of yarn and then double up the thread. Make the pompoms using a small washer as a template or make one from cardboard by drawing round a small coin. If you cannot make a pompom, buttons or beads in matching colours will look just as effective.

Useful Addresses
& Acknowledgements

Suppliers of Rowan Yarns

Australia
Rowan at Sunspun
185 Canterbury Road
Canterbury
Victoria 3126
Tel: 03 9830 1609

Canada
Diamond Yarn
9697 St Laurent
Montreal
Quebec H3L 2N1
Tel: 514 388 6188

UK
Rowan Yarns
Green Mill Lane
Holmfirth
West Yorkshire
HD9 2DX
Tel: 01484 681881
www.knitrowan.com

USA
Westminster Fibers, Inc.
3 Northern Boulevard, Suite 3
Amherst
New Hampshire 03031
Tel: 603 886 5041

Bear Materials

For ½ inch (4mm) bead eyes:
GJ Beads
Units 1&3
Court Arcade
The Wharf
St Ives
Cornwall
TR26 1LG

For looped-back eyes, tiny buttons
and bear accessories:
Melanie's Little Bear Co.
Unit 29
The Strand
First Floor
Bromsgrove
Worcestershire
B61 8AB
01527 459746
www.melsbears.co.uk

Admiral Bears
37 Warren Drive
Ruislip
Middlesex
HA4 9RD
020 8868 9598
www.admiral-bears.com

Author's Acknowledgements
I would like to thank the following people for their help in making this book possible; Kandy Regis, knitting editor of the *Woman's Weekly* magazine, for giving me advice and encouragement to make a book and Kate Kirby (former Editorial Director of Collins & Brown) for liking my teds enough to agree to the book being published.

My family, friends and colleagues for their help, especially my close friends Dawn and Chris Bates for their continual support and encouragement. My mother Maureen and Tracey Shillito for patiently knitting up my designs as they evolved.

My husband John and daughters Catherine and Elizabeth for understanding when I had too much to do and knitted teddies were more important than Sunday lunch.

A big thank you also to Nicola Hodgson, senior editor, for all her help, Sian Irvine and Michael Wicks for the photography, Zeta Jones, for designing the book, and Marilyn Wilson and Katie Hardwicke for proofreading the patterns and text.